From Rock Around the Clock to TikTok

Eighty Years of Life, Learning and Hope

Memphis Central High Classmates of 1959

ISBN: 978-1-66785-903-3 (paperback)

ISBN: 978-1-66785-904-0 (eBook)

CONTENTS

INTRODUCTION

This is a book full of memories. Eighty years on Earth leaves you with a lot of them. We are fourteen classmates who all attended the same high school -- Central High School in Memphis, Tennessee, and graduated in 1959. We were born in 1940 and 1941, and we turned eighty in 2020 and 2021. When the coronavirus pandemic hit a few months after our sixtieth high school reunion in 2019, a couple of us started to meet up for video calls on Zoom. Then a few more joined in. It was informal, and spontaneous, just like when groups of us randomly met up as teenagers to go to a movie on a Saturday afternoon. Having our whole class participate in a cyber class reunion wasn't the goal. It was just catching up with a few old friends who happened to come together during a worldwide lockdown. We ended up meeting about twice a month and sharing stories from our lives. A few months in, we realized that we had lived through a lot of momentous events, and each of us had an insider perspective on at least one of them through the years.

That's when we got the idea to write them down and make them into this book. If people from the senior class of 1859 had done this when they were eighty, they would have told about graduating two years before the Civil War, witnessing the eras of Reconstruction and Jim Crow, experiencing the inventions of the electric lightbulb, the phonograph, airplanes, cars, radio, and TV. They would talk of World War I, and Black people and women getting the right to vote, the building of the railroads, Prohibition, and the dawn of the Jazz Age. Our experience 100 years later has echoes of similar, significant upheavals, changes and advancements.

We were born during World War II. We grew up during the Korean War and the start of the civil rights movement. We witnessed the birth of rock and roll in our hometown. We went to segregated schools and graduated two years before thirteen Black elementary school students began to desegregate Memphis public schools. Some of us fought in Vietnam. We also lived through the women's liberation movement, the availability of the first, FDA-approved, birth control pill, and we had to come to terms with the assassination of Martin Luther King, Jr. in our hometown. We experienced the moon landing, Watergate, and 9/11, along with the birth of personal computers, overnight package delivery, the internet, smart phones, and social media. And through it all, we adapted and adopted new ways of doing business, having relationships and families, and even keeping in touch with old friends.

Our stories are here for the generations. We are a varied and accomplished group, including professors, engineers, doctors, businesspeople, mothers and fathers, entrepreneurs, teachers, and a filmmaker. And we all want to point out that there are others from our large high school class whose stories aren't in this book, but who have also done impressive things and have wonderful stories to tell. So, we didn't attempt to make any major, comprehensive statements, or advance any sweeping theories about the world, politics, religion, humanity, or our whole generation. We just wanted to share our particular stories, from our hearts.

The book is structured so that each person's story opens with a momentous event in history in which they had some firsthand participation, or a personal milestone that illustrates a larger trend in the world at the time. The stories are ordered chronologically. Each starts with a short, bullet point description of that lead event, denoting when (and sometimes where) it occurred. So the first story in the book begins when our classmate learns his big brother was killed in the Korean War. A few stories later, a classmate shares what it was like being a student at Ole Miss when James Meredith became the first Black person to attend the university. One of our classmates worked at NASA during the moon landing. Another classmate was one of the first women sportscasters hired at a national television network. We share business and political victories, and some defeats. We span the globe with stories from all across the United States to the Middle East and the Far East. Each storyteller then backtracks to share more about their unique life trajectory.

We don't talk much about high school in these stories. We left that to our Zoom calls and class reunions. Instead, we tried to take our collective memories from eighty years on Earth and give a homegrown and time-tested view of the ups and downs of our lives, and of the rich moments in between. We hope you enjoy them. And we hope our stories serve generations to come, who might want to know how lives were lived and what people thought and did in the last half of the twentieth century and the first quarter of the twenty-first century.

1 - John Huggins

1953 - The Korean War

In late March of 1953, my family went more than a week without hearing from Brother. But no one talked about what might have kept him from writing his usual, weekly letter to us. Then, one morning around 8, as I was getting ready for school and mother was getting ready for work, we heard a knock at our front door. Standing on the front porch were two Army officers. They were bringing us the news of Brother's death in Korea.

Whenever any of our relatives spoke of Brother, we all knew they were talking about Kenon A. Huggins Jr., my big brother. He was killed in action, serving in the Korean War as a lieutenant and Army field artillery officer.

I had heard that when my Uncle Bud came home from the Army during World War II, he just walked down the street to our house one day, unannounced. He'd been discharged from duty, and none of the family knew when he would arrive. I guess that's what I imagined for Brother when his time of service ended. However, that was not to be. His wife and two children were left alone. My mother had lost a son, and me a brother and my own father figure. What a blow that such a fine man was gone.

I don't recall my actual father being with us when I was growing up, because he decided to leave before my memories even began forming as a child. And he never came back. Brother was born twelve years before I was. So, I looked up to him, like he was my father. He would take me to Crump Stadium to watch the Central High football games, and to the Mid-South Fair and Rodeo. Those were lasting memories for me as a little boy.

My mother had served our country in WWII as a "Rosie the Riveter" -- one of the women recruited to work on vital defense production lines. I didn't hear much else about her war experiences, but I believe she worked in a defense plant in the Memphis area.

Through my childhood, several of my aunts, uncles, and cousins lived with us part of the time, or we moved in with them, since my mother couldn't afford to own a house of her own after my father left. That was very enjoyable for me since I had cousins to play with who were around my age. Eventually, my mother began working at the locally famous clothing store called Helen of Memphis, and she became the manager of the children's department. Then, she was able to buy a home on Harbert, between Rembert and Tanglewood in Midtown. I went to Idlewild Elementary. At that time, my brother had graduated from Central High and was on his own, working and then getting married. My older sister, Martha, attended Central High then too. We didn't have a car. But I remember occasionally going downtown on the bus with my mother and eating at Britlings Cafeteria. I always got the spaghetti.

A year later, my mother sold that house and purchased another one out east, near Memphis State University on Patterson Street. So, our family moved and I began third grade at the Memphis State Training School, where education students from Memphis State would do their student teaching. I stayed there for elementary and junior high school, through the ninth grade. The faculty was excellent and the experience for both the students and student teachers was truly remarkable. The school was small. There were only two homeroom classes at each grade level. I think our entire ninth grade class was probably no more than fifty students.

I remember our telephone service was on a party line. When you went to make a phone call you just might be picking up the phone on a neighbor's conversation. When we got our first television, all us kids would sit on the floor up close to the TV while the adults sat in chairs or couches across the room. This was the reason my mother saw fit to have my eyes tested. As a result, I began wearing glasses in fourth grade, and for the rest of my life. Later, when I joined the Air Force, my poor eyesight kept me from qualifying for pilot training.

During high school, I remember we danced a lot on Wink Martindale's Dance Party TV show on WHBQ-TV and in the Central High gym at sock hop parties. I was in for a bit of a shock when I got to high school and realized I was one of many in a class that was about 500 strong -- a far cry from the fifty or so classmates at my elementary and junior high school. Also, the Central student body was as much of a mixture of backgrounds and religions as I had ever experienced. The bulk of the students were Christians, but there was a sizeable presence of Jewish classmates. It was my first experience with the Jewish culture, and I have remained thankful for the opportunity. We had no Black students, because all schools in Memphis, public or private, were still racially segregated in the 1950s. It wasn't until I was in the Air Force that I had any real experience with racial integration.

Central had no Catholic students because they all went to the various Catholic high schools in Memphis. Since we lived so far out in East Memphis, I had to ride the city bus to school most of the time. I would catch the bus in front of my house and ride all the way down to Bellevue Street and walk up the street to Central High. On occasion, a Catholic high school girl would board the bus at Highland and ride down to Immaculate

Conception Catholic girls' school at Central and Belvedere. Sometimes she would be wearing her cheerleader uniform for one of the Catholic boys' high schools. I always thought I should meet her and strike up a conversation, but I never did approach her.

I was thirteen years old when I got my first job working as a carhop at an ice house on the corner of Southern and Highland Street, which sold fresh block ice and bagged crushed ice, along with a selection of cold drinks and limited grocery items. My job was to meet the customers at their car windows, take their orders, collect their money, and deliver the items to their cars. This was a summertime job, and the side benefit came when we got to cool off in the freezing icehouse where we went to fetch ice for the customers. We could always find excuses to go in the icehouse just to cool off. My working career began there at what seemed like an awesome pay rate of 33 cents per hour. From that point on, I always worked while in school, in the summer during high school, and all year round when I was in college.

The job I disliked the most was selling women's shoes at Baker's in downtown Memphis during the Christmas break from high school. I also managed to work as an air conditioning repair serviceman helper, a clerk at a convenience store, and a gas island jockey at the East Memphis Sears department store. The most dangerous job I ever held was as a cab driver when the Yellow Cab Company had a driver strike in Memphis. Several fraternity brothers at Memphis State and I decided to drive as scabs during the strike. We drove for several weeks and did make some pretty good money. I personally was never threatened, but when one of my buddies received a threat, we all decided we had done enough, so we all quit.

The time at Memphis State really set the stage for the rest of my life. As I began my freshman year, the university initiated racial integration. As far as I knew, the eight Black students who attended the university my first year were treated with respect. This was in apparent contrast to the problems at Ole Miss just sixty miles south, where James Meredith's enrollment as the first Black student caused white students on campus to riot. I believe the reason our integration went more smoothly was because our deans and our university president made certain that the white students understood there would be no tolerance of any conflict or strife.

Lynn and I began dating in our junior year. By the time we graduated, we were engaged to be married. It turned out that the girl I'd seen on the bus every day going to Central but never spoke to was Gail O'Donnell, and she was in Lynn's sorority. We became friends, and Lynn and I palled around with her in college. In fact, she was a bridesmaid in our wedding and Lynn was a bridesmaid in her wedding. Our families have kept up with each other through the years, including attending each other's fiftieth wedding anniversaries. My college studies were concentrated in chemistry, biology, math, and physics. Lynn studied business and education.

When we graduated, I had a high number on the Army draft list for the Vietnam War, which meant I was likely to be drafted. The war was really heating up then. Many of my classmates were getting married because it could get you a draft deferment. Lynn and I decided that I should go ahead and volunteer for the Air Force and apply to officer training, rather than hurry up and get married just to get a deferment. We could spend four years in the Air Force and avoid the chance of my being drafted into the Army.

It was also in the back of my mind that this was another incident in which Brother was protecting me, in effect. I had heard of a Defense Department policy that any family that had lost a son in combat would not allow a sole surviving son from that family to serve in an active combat area. In my mind, Brother was still looking out for me.

In September of 1963, I left for Officer Training School at Lackland Air Force Base in San Antonio, Texas. One of my squadron mates was a fellow named Brad Near, from Arizona, and he already had his pilot's license, having done some contract flying into remote locations in Arizona and Mexico. He immediately joined the Lackland AFB Aero Club so he could rent aircraft. He would take me flying around Texas on the weekends. On one occasion, we rented a T6 training aircraft to fly down to Corpus Christi and the Texas coast. My friend was skilled at landing on beaches, and we thought we could go explore Padre Island on our excursion. We flew to the Texas coast and began looking for a place to land the plane. We spotted an old deserted road about 100 yards from the beach on Padre Island. My friend put the plane down on this road, and we walked through a cotton field to get to the beach. When we emerged from the field and onto the beach, I told my friend to watch where he was stepping through the cotton because he had just stepped right next to a coiled rattlesnake. The blood drained from his face and he insisted that when we went back to the plane I should be in front, because if one of us were to be bitten by a snake it should be me, not him. His logic was sound since he was the only one who could fly us out of a bad situation, just not so good for me. Luckily, the trip back to Lackland went without any incidents.

Also, during my officer training, it was shortly after lunch one day in 1963 when we were in a classroom lecture on leadership. Suddenly, an Air Force officer entered the classroom unannounced. He took control of the class and made the announcement that President Kennedy had just been shot in Dallas. He informed us that all classes were cancelled, and to immediately return to our barracks for the remainder of the day. He added that all Air Force units were being placed on alert.

Just before our training class was to receive our commissions, I was called into a private meeting and offered the option of becoming a regular commission officer, rather than a reserve commission officer. This was an opportunity to make the Air Force a career. I was honored to be asked since this was offered to very few in Officer Training School. But since our plans for a future married life did not include a career in the Air Force, I turned it down.

The first assignment of my reserve commission was to attend communications officer school at Keesler AFB in Biloxi, Mississippi. This was a year-long training school assignment. Lynn was teaching in Memphis. So, when her school year ended in June 1964, we got married in her hometown of Osceola, Arkansas. Then we moved to Biloxi, which was a very laid-back place. I would go to class for six hours a day, which left plenty of daylight hours to go to the beach or go fishing. As a young married couple, we enjoyed the leisurely pace. Also, we enjoyed the officers club for playing bridge and for happy hour on Friday night, with 25-cent shrimp and nickel beer.

In December 1964, our class graduated from communications school. I received my first real working assignment to Offutt AFB, in Omaha, Nebraska -- the headquarters of the Strategic Air Command (SAC). My unit was the First Aerospace Communications Group.

SAC was the premier strategic force for the United States in the cold war. The mission of SAC was to provide worldwide instant nuclear strike capability through our 24-hour alert B52 Bomber fleet and its U.S. land-based Minuteman Missile force. The base was loaded with top brass Air Force general officers and even a Navy admiral representing the Navy's nuclear submarine fleet. Our group was responsible for all SAC communications and for providing the communications battle staff officers for the underground SAC command post as well as the SAC airborne command post. My early assignments had me coordinating communications developments at many other national command centers such as the Headquarters of AT&T in New York City, the Pentagon, the National Military Command Center at Fort Detrick, Maryland, and the Air Defense Command (NORAD) at Cheyenne Mountain, Colorado.

I was promoted to captain and was assigned to the SAC HQ battle staff as a communications officer. This position was a 24-hour manned position in the underground SAC command post, and a 24-hour manned position on the Airborne SAC command post. Our responsibilities were to keep communications functioning between the command post and all the SAC forces worldwide. The SAC missile force was in constant communication with the SAC command post, ready to receive orders to launch their missiles at any time, in case of a nuclear attack. The airborne command post had missile launch capability in the event that all SAC command post communication was lost to any missile site. The operations officer and the communications officer had a missile launch panel at our positions. We could launch any missile from the aircraft if all missile controls on the ground were to fail. For this responsibility I had to go through special missile training at Vandenburg AFB at Lompoc, California. It definitely gave me pause to consider the consequences of my new responsibility.

Up until then, my duties were strictly support, with no direct responsibility for releasing the use of deadly, world-ending force. I had to realize that I held the keys to the possible annihilation of the enemy, but also the subsequent destruction of my own country and family. This was quite sobering and caused me to fully internalize the true deadly nature of this responsibility.

A tragic incident happened while I was on duty in the underground command post. SAC forces were generally not involved in the Vietnam War, since our mission was nuclear deterrence and Vietnam had no nuclear weapons. But toward the end of the war, SAC was called upon to make bombing runs over Vietnam using our B52 bombers and dropping conventional weapons. The B52s would fly out of Guam in the western Pacific Ocean to make their bomb runs over Vietnam and return to base at Guam. One evening, there came an announcement that two B52s had collided on their return flight to Guam. On board was a SAC major general who had been riding in the jump seat during the mission. His plane went down. That night, we lost one of the highest-ranking officers to die in the Vietnam War. Many of the SAC officers personally knew the general and said he was one of the best. It was a sad time in the command post.

Even amid the trials of wartime, there were some lighter, happier times too. Lynn and I were glad to serve at Offutt. The amenities offered were of such high quality because of all the top brass on base. The officers club and the officer club swimming pool were great for us newlyweds. And we will always think fondly of that time, because our first child, John Jr., was born at the base hospital at Offutt. Lynn particularly enjoyed taking him to the pool. The social life with fellow officers and their wives was fantastic. Also, at Offutt, I was able to experience the real gifts of an integrated society in my life, because one of my best bosses there was an African American major.

In January of 1968, Lynn and our young son, Jay, left Offutt and the Air Force to return to Memphis to settle down. I had to look for a job. This was the dawn of business computers and the development of modern business systems, which was to be my chosen career. I landed a job with W. R. Grace, a major New York conglomerate and chemical firm with a new agricultural chemicals division to be headquartered in Memphis. The immediate task was to establish a computer center in Memphis to serve the division manufacturing and sales offices covering all states east of the Rockies. There were major production facilities in Trinidad, North Carolina, Florida, Tennessee, Texas, and Iowa.

In Memphis, my personal life revolved around my family. Lynn and I bought a home on the GI Bill, and we had two more children, Jennifer in 1969 and Jean Clare in 1975. Jennifer had a congenital health problem which required us to rely on the Mayo Clinic in Rochester, Minnesota, for initial diagnosis and care. Having Jennifer treated at Mayo was an awesome experience, since they were the premier experts on her condition. Also, we were assisted by an old Central High classmate, Sarah Pickens, whose husband, Dr. Robert Waller, was the CEO of the Mayo Clinic. Sarah and Robert had all of us -- Lynn, me, and our three children -- over to their home and helped us navigate the facilities at the clinic. We came and went to the clinic for several treatments and surgeries during the next twenty years.

In 1975, I got a master's degree in Management and Math at Memphis State. A few years later, I signed on as a systems coordinator for Martin

Marietta Aerospace at the NASA Michoud production facility in New Orleans. The Michoud plant manufactured the external tank for the NASA Space Shuttle. It was then transported to Cape Canaveral by barge via the intercoastal waterway. The production schedule called for one external tank per month to be finished and shipped. My role was to coordinate the development of specific computer systems for support of the facilities planning group.

Our time in New Orleans was a great experience for Lynn and the children. We lived in a neighborhood of natives of the city and transplanted young families. We joined a nearby swim and racquet club and had lots of access to the rivers, bayous, and lakes around New Orleans. I got in some fishing, and we were close enough to visit the Florida Gulf Coast frequently for beach time. We enjoyed several seasons of Mardi Gras with the parades and parties -- although in South Louisiana there is always a reason to hold a party or *fais do-do* (Cajun for party). We also ate our share of boiled crawfish, shrimp, and raw oysters on the half-shell while in New Orleans.

Later in the 1980s, we moved back to Memphis, where I became a consultant, providing operational improvements to financial institutions. Our clients were nationwide, from New York to Montana to Florida, and dozens of states in between.

Next was the phase of our married life when we put our three children through college. Our son went to the University of Memphis and our two daughters went to Ole Miss. During this time Lynn was working at State Technical Institute junior college, and she went back to the University of Memphis to get her master's degree in Instructional Design. After graduating, our oldest daughter got her master's degree in Occupational Therapy at Belmont University. None of our kids ended up in Memphis but scattered through the South, with Jay in Richmond, Virginia, Jennifer in Decatur, Georgia, and Jean Clare in Hot Springs, Arkansas.

My final career move was to Memphis-based FedEx, in their technology division. Our group was responsible for ensuring that all new systems met FedEx standards for technology and software. The systems were reviewed for compliance before allowing newly developed software and hardware to be put to use by anyone across the FedEx organization. I also served in an intercompany exchange group with various corporations nationwide, in unrelated industries so that no member would be a direct competitor of any other member. We served with people from General Motors, Raytheon, Chevron, and Wells Fargo, among others. Each of us presented on current topics of interest within technology, focused on challenges that all members were experiencing. On one occasion, our group did a presentation on the importance of technology at FedEx. We directly quoted our CEO, Fred Smith. Using his mantra that "information about the package is as important as the package itself," we showed how technology we developed gave customers what they were really looking for from a company -- not just good products, but also good service and clear, timely, useful communication.

I retired from FedEx in 2008, but thanks to the excellent education I received from elementary school through high school and college, and in the military and graduate school, I was able to face the challenges of the business world with confidence and a firm belief that hard work brings great rewards.

John Huggins, fly fishing, 2008   John and Lynn Huggins and family, 50th Anniversary, June 13, 2014

2 - Doug Meeks

1957 & 1958 - Little Rock Central High Integration

By the end of my junior year at Central High in 1958, I had a sense I was being prepared for what lay ahead, however unclear that was at the time. I had already decided I wanted to be in the clergy, and I was becoming fairly certain that I wanted to be an academic as well. So for me, Central was the place where my profession began to come into view. Central was a stable, much-respected institution, which I esteemed from my first day there -- although the first two weeks of football practice in the relentless Memphis heat of August made me want to be almost anywhere else.

Playing football and basketball was as important to me growing up as the rest of my school and church experience. And I had high expectations of making a contribution to what we all hoped would be Central's football and basketball championships in my senior year. But during the fourth football game of that season, I suffered a broken leg on the field, and I faced broken dreams in my mind of being part of any sports triumphs that year.

After the injury, I still traveled with the football team. A major turning point came for me while I sat on the bench during the game against Little Rock Central High School in the fall of 1958. Our football coach, Ruffner Murray, had wanted us to play other "great Central high schools in the South," such as in Little Rock and Chattanooga. The year before, we had played Little Rock, and I was almost unconscious at the time of what had happened there just a few weeks before in the fall of 1957. I don't remember much about the 1957 game either, except the sound beating we got. But in 1958, the significance of having played Little Rock Central the year before began to sink in. I was thinking and feeling a bit more deeply than ever before about a lot of things as a senior, perhaps because of the broken leg. So, I was struck that an event with global significance had taken place on the Little Rock Central campus in September 1957, and I couldn't escape its implications.

The "Little Rock Nine" were the Black students who bravely tested the 1954 Supreme Court ruling *Brown v. Board of Education* that had made segregation in public schools unconstitutional. In the fall of 1957, the Arkansas governor, Orval Faubus, attempted to block the students from entering Central with the National Guard, but President Eisenhower sent federal troops to uphold the new federal policy. Sitting on that bench a year later, even a "protected" high school student from a still segregated high school in Memphis like me began to see the justice in desegregation, and from then on I followed the Civil Rights Movement more closely.

As I look back, it seems that crucial junctures of my life have been marked by events in the African American struggle for civil rights. While in that cast in the fall of 1958, I did a lot of reading. I particularly remember reading Faulkner's *Light in August* for the first time. I was fascinated and deeply disturbed by it. For a while I wished I had not read it. I was awakening to the suffering in the history and culture of Memphis and the South that had been shaping me all along.

I also read Twain's *Huckleberry Finn* that year, though I certainly didn't fully comprehend it on first reading. Huck and Jim's trip on a raft down the Mississippi opened my eyes to issues of race. But it took me some time to learn that white supremacy is not exclusively a Memphis or Southern problem but rather suffuses all of Western history. Those who displaced the Native peoples and "settled" America brought their white racism with them -- the Spanish, the French, and above all, my English forebears. I now see white supremacy as a special brand of the original sin: pride.

In my senior year, a sadness fell over me as I realized that Memphis had thrived as a marketplace for two intertwined commodities -- cotton and enslaved people. I began to see that the orthodox Southern stories of the "Lost Cause" covered up the human scourge of slavery with "states' rights" politics and legalities. And, even worse, a tortured interpretation of the Bible, ancient Rome, and medieval chivalry painted a picture of Southern culture, especially plantation culture, that was a lie.

Many times, driving past the handsome, massive statue of Nathan Bedford Forrest in a park in downtown Memphis, I wondered why the city had paid him such a tribute. Later, I learned that while he was one of the most elevated generals in the South's "Lost Cause" movement, he was also a cotton plantation owner, an enslaver, and a major seller of enslaved people in Memphis, and he was among the most vilified Civil War criminals. His troops perpetrated the horrendous mass slaughter of Black and white Union troops at Fort Pillow just north of Memphis.

Ever since my senior year at Central, I have had mixed feelings toward Memphis: an aversion to aspects of its history and a love for what is best in its culture. Later on, I realized that I am a product of the place that is located between William Faulkner's fictional Yoknapatawpha County in the delta of northern Mississippi and Mark Twain's Hannibal with its Mississippi riverboats steaming toward New Orleans. I began to be aware that my home city was fraught with tears. As Faulkner said, "The past is not dead. It is not even past."

Jerry Manley, a friend at my side in many ways in those high school days, drove me to Oxford (our family had only one car, and that had to be used for work) to meet with Coach Vaught, who had been calling for several weeks to assure me that Ole Miss was where I should play football. But while on the beautiful Ole Miss campus, I had a strange sensation of Faulkner's divided soul: wounded by the economics and culture of cotton plantations and slavery, but unalterably a son of the South. I decided to play football and study at Vanderbilt, which seemed to this Memphian a good place to flee. I also decided to major in English literature.

But Vandy didn't feel just right.

As is well known, Vanderbilt is not a football powerhouse. But that fall, at least the freshman team had made a good showing in Neyland Stadium in Knoxville against the University of Tennessee. The vaunted UT single-wing was formidable, and as it came toward me, I took a cleat which opened a gash in my eyebrow. It was sewn up in the Volunteers' locker room. But a Volunteer germ somehow entered the wound, and when I returned to Nashville, I had to stay three days in the Vanderbilt hospital with an infection. (No bad feelings, though, because my little brother John later played for UT, after having been captain of Central's football team when Central did win the championship.) Also, I was learning more about Nathan Bedford Forrest, and how he played a part not only in dismantling Reconstruction and initiating the Ku Klux Klan, but also in the founding of my university fraternity. After that, I lost my zeal for Greek life on campus.

But the deciding event of my fate came during my freshman year. The peacefulness of the magnolia-covered Vanderbilt campus was broken when Rev. James Lawson, an African American graduate student from Ohio, who entered Vanderbilt Divinity School as only the second Black student to attend Vanderbilt, was expelled. A gifted intellect with sharp leadership abilities, Rev. Lawson had become a leader of the famous

Nashville lunch counter sit-ins for civil rights in the 1960s and was one of the chief advisors of Martin Luther King, Jr. while still a student. In reaction to the sit-ins, a member of the Vanderbilt Board of Trustees made untrue allegations against Lawson, and the board was persuaded to ask for his dismissal. When the Chancellor agreed and carried out the dismissal, the dean of the Divinity School, under whose care I had been put by my bishop, called me in. He said, "I am resigning in protest, three-fourths of the faculty are leaving, and you should, too." I was very green and didn't fully understand what had become an enormous disruption in the university (which in many ways it is still trying to mend). I had come to play football and to get an education. This was a time of deep uncertainty for me. But I saw the path I needed to take and decided to leave Vanderbilt.

The Lawson affair and my slowly arriving realization that I had to choose between football and what it was going to take to prepare for ordained life in the church and a life of research and teaching in the academy led me to decide to return to Memphis and accept the offer of Southwestern at Memphis (now Rhodes College) to take me in.

It was a good decision -- first of all because Southwestern is where I met my wife, Blair. I was bowled over by her and was very soon convinced that I wanted to spend my life with her, though it took her longer to have a reciprocal conviction. When Blair and I became committed to each other, my study habits and grades improved considerably. We were in several English classes together and sometimes shared her textbooks, which I couldn't afford. We spent hours together in the library. We have been "cleaving" to each other (as the King Jimmy version of the Bible puts it) ever since. The relationship we developed in college has blossomed into many creative endeavors, as Blair became a partner in my life with students and my research and writing. She is my editor in the broad sense of that word. Over the years my students have tolerated me, but they have loved Blair. She has published five books in the area of liturgy.

The great gift of Southwestern as a liberal arts college was that it planted me in the biblical literature and the culture of Western civilization. I sensed continuity with the glimmers I had felt at Central of communion with great thinkers who belonged to many centuries in the past. The faculty held in creative tension this critical devotion to tradition and the rising importance of the STEM disciplines. Einstein said, "Science can tell us what we *can* do but not what we *should* do." Southwestern was a quiet oasis in Memphis, and it was just what I needed to begin to make up my mind about what was true in the past and what the past could and should mean for the troublesome events taking place in Memphis and everywhere at that time.

In the first week of June 1963, Blair and I graduated on Monday, got married on Wednesday, and drove 500 miles for me to preach on Sunday. We were already in the next phase of our long educational odyssey, since my work that summer as assistant pastor in the Clifton Forge Methodist Church in Virginia was an internship for Duke University Divinity School. From that fall of 1963, we were at Duke for five years -- three years of Divinity School, and two years of PhD course work. For the most part these were happy and fulfilling years in which I sensed a steady flow between high school, college, and my young adult life in graduate school.

The Divinity School was physically and culturally at the center of the university. Being at a research university with a growing international reputation and a cosmopolitan student body offered a stimulating lifestyle -- although, in the first few weeks of our arriving at Duke, life was sobered by several events. On Sunday, September 15, 1963, just two weeks into the first semester, four Ku Klux Klan members planted nineteen sticks of dynamite under the 16th Street Baptist Church in Birmingham, Alabama. This white supremacist terrorist bombing killed four African American girls attending Sunday School, an act that Martin Luther King, Jr. described as "one of the most vicious and tragic crimes perpetrated against humanity." Only seven weeks later, I was sitting at my desk in our apartment concentrating on a theological text when a phone call came from a friend saying that President

Kennedy had been assassinated. These two killings shook me as no killing had. But sadly, they were only the first in a train of violence lasting through today, the violence intimated to me in my reading of Faulkner in my senior year at Central. It started my wrestling with the theodicy question: "If God is good, how could such evil happen?"

The Duke days were also the days of the Vietnam War. I was so opposed to the irrationality of the politics that had brought on the killing of some of my friends in that war. They had been sent to a bloody sacrifice. Some days I was not sure what I would do if my brother in Vietnam or my brother-in-law in Thailand were killed. In one of the trips Duke friends and I took to Washington in opposition to the war, we spent an afternoon in the office of North Carolina Senator Sam Ervin, who, though he defended segregation laws, stood up for civil rights against Joseph McCarthy and later the Watergate offenders. He listened all afternoon patiently and, it seemed to me, with some empathy for our arguments against the war, his famous eyebrows bouncing up and down. At the conclusion, he posed only one question, "How many votes did you bring with you today?" At that moment, I learned both the fragility of democracy and the urgency of defending it.

The last two years of my graduate time at Duke were filled with hard work and good surprises. As a graduate teaching assistant, I assumed more teaching responsibilities with my own seminars in theology and preaching. Then in 1967 and 1968, I was appointed as assistant to Jürgen Moltmann, a visiting professor from Germany. When he arrived in September, he was just beginning to be widely known by Americans, helped by a front-page article in the *New York Times* about the way his *Theology of Hope* had caught on in Europe and was catching on in America. Blair and I set to work helping him and his wife, Elisabeth, also a theologian, and their four daughters get oriented to Durham and the South.

Their great sense of humor was invaluable as they adjusted to Southern culture. My job was to help prepare his lectures and help lead his seminar, to consult with students, and to take over his seminar on Christology when he returned to Germany in April. I helped in the organization of a very large conference the first week of April in 1968, on Moltmann's theology of hope. Many of the leading American theologians were invited. It was a conference full of enlightened and heated discussion. On the last night, someone rushed into the auditorium and shouted, "Martin Luther King has been shot and killed." Deadly silence fell on the whole proceedings and my heart sank: Dr. King, murdered in my hometown, Memphis. How could this be? I wasn't certain I would ever recover from the loss and the shame.

The next day, Black students from the historically Black North Carolina Central University came to the Duke campus, and with Duke students, sat on the ground in long rows for three days in the big quad in front of Duke Chapel. On the first day, long lines of Black and white students danced through the rows hand-in-hand. That the university officials supported the demonstrations changed the atmosphere, if only enough to begin serious discussion.

The rest of 1968 played out to become what I think of as a watershed year. Nothing has been the same since. There was the April 4th assassination of Martin Luther King, Jr. Then in June, the murder of Bobby Kennedy. In July were the Paris student barricades. In August was the invasion of Czechoslovakia and the violence at the Democratic National Convention. And finally in November, the election of Richard Nixon. The only real bright spot for us was that our first son was born on August 23.

By the end of 1968, it was time for our family to move to Germany, where I had been awarded a Fulbright Fellowship at Tübingen University from 1968 to 1970. Exhausted and spiritually depleted, we boarded a Lufthansa flight and took off for two years in Germany.

Tübingen University was where Jürgen Moltmann taught. He welcomed us to his country and his academic home, as we had welcomed him when he was at Duke. The university was established in 1477. It was influenced in its early history by Melanchthon, the associate of Martin Luther in the Protestant Reformation. It is known for many scientists, such as Kepler, and key figures in philosophy such as Hölderlin, Schelling, and Hegel. By the end of the 1960s, it had become the theological Mecca for Christianity. Theological students and professors from all over the world came there to study with probably the most famous Protestant theologian of today, our friend and colleague Jürgen Moltmann, and the most famous Catholic theologian, Hans Küng. While we were in Tübingen there were 150 foreign scholars in residence in the Protestant faculty alone. Joseph Ratzinger, who later became Pope Benedict XVI, was also on the Catholic faculty. But he did not find the lively atmosphere of student revolt to his liking, and he departed for Munich in my second year. We, on the other hand, did like the open, energetic feeling among the students and the lively discussions about how the university could meet the challenges of a culture that had to deal with the past of Nazism and the Holocaust. Some aspects of the university's medieval academic traditions seemed to me to offer more freedom to deal with the thorniest issues of the day than the increasingly top-heavy administration in American universities.

The effects of World War II could still be seen in Tübingen then. It is located in the southwest sector of Germany, which was controlled by the French during and after the war. Tübingen's old medieval market square and castle were at the center of the city. That was our first view of old Europe and led to our extensive travels all over Europe during those two years. We've always been grateful that an academic life afforded us the opportunity to travel widely.

My research for the Fulbright Commission was on political theology, which by then had developed in Germany and throughout Europe. It was during my time there that I began to see the relationship between theology, politics, and the economy, and that has been a primary focus of my research ever since.

We returned to the United States in the summer of 1970 and prepared to take up my first teaching post at Huntingdon College, a small liberal arts college in Montgomery, Alabama. For eight months, I taught Bible and Philosophy there. Returning to the American South after two years in Europe was the biggest cultural shock of our lives. The old signals of leftover Jim Crow were more subtle, but omnipresent. Huntingdon had a distinguished history, but at that time it was paternalistic and determined to keep the old Southern ways. I loved my students, and they loved our toddler son as Blair strolled with him on campus. Many of my students were struggling as well, with what they were learning in relation to their place in society, in a setting that had become frozen in its ideology.

Our shock was alleviated in many ways by Rev. Dr. Murray Branch and his wife Mima Branch. Murray was the successor of Martin Luther King, Jr. at Dexter Avenue Baptist Church, which is located across from the Alabama state capitol. He was also a professor of Old Testament at the Interdenominational Theological Center in Atlanta, a consortium of several African American seminaries. Murray invited me to preach at Dexter Avenue Church, and I learned a lot about Martin Luther King, Jr. Dr. King had done his doctoral course work at Boston University. He decided to accept Dexter Avenue's call to be their pastor because he thought it would be a quiet place to complete his doctoral dissertation in an undemanding congregation among some professional people, lawyers, and insurance company executives. I learned it was not King who began the civil rights movement in Montgomery. Two generations of railroad porters, domestic workers, and laborers had been building the groundwork for the civil rights movement. Martin's education at Boston University School of Theology had prepared him to be a leader in church and society. He knew the Scripture. He knew church history. He knew ethics. And he certainly knew how to speak publicly. But he didn't have the courage at first to step into a highly dangerous leadership role. Courage it seems can't be taught by books and lectures. It was the people of the congregation and the city, some without much education, who gave him the courage to stand up and who held him up when the threats against him multiplied. When Rosa Parks kept her seat in the "white" section of the bus, Martin was ready to step or be pushed forward in leadership. I've always hoped that my teaching of theology would prepare my students also to step forward.

Dr. Branch and I began an interracial, interdenominational clergy group that met at our apartment on campus. It made the college administration nervous. I had forgotten that I was no longer in Europe. We got in trouble publicly when we spoke out against the plight of domestic workers at the military base south of Montgomery. The officers from the North did not want to give up paying exploitative wages to their "help."

Around that same time, in January of 1971, Blair gave birth to our second son in a hospital that, sadly, did not allow fathers in the delivery room and discouraged breastfeeding. From her hospital window Blair could see each morning two Black men struggling in the cold wind as they raised the Confederate flag on the capitol's pinnacle. It struck us both as an ultimate affront. In April we departed Montgomery, but after we were gone for a while, we were glad for the education we received there.

In February of 1971, I had received a call to join the faculty of Eden Theological Seminary in St. Louis. The seminary was named for a railroad station near where it was first established in the nineteenth century, not for the garden in the Bible. It was originally the seminary of the old Evangelical (Lutheran) denomination in Germany. Then, when the Evangelicals united with the German Reformed Church in the United States, it became an Evangelical and Reformed seminary. Finally, when the E&Rs united with the Congregational Church to form the United Church of Christ, Eden became a seminary of the UCC. Eden is probably best known for Reinhold Niebuhr, the most widely acclaimed American theologian of the twentieth century, and his brother H. Richard Niebuhr, arguably the most influential American theology professor of the twentieth century. Both were students at Eden. Richard was also a faculty member and dean at Eden before going to Yale in the 1930s. When I came to Eden in the fall of 1970, the Niebuhr brothers' afterglow was still palpable.

I was back on the Mississippi River -- this time closer to Mark Twain's Hannibal. Jürgen Moltmann visited us in every place we have lived. He quipped that he baptized our first son, Douglas, in Tübingen with Neckar River water and our second son, John, in St. Louis with Mississippi River water. Every time Jürgen came to St. Louis, we spent an evening on a Mississippi riverboat with a good dinner and afterward scotch, cigars, and dancing. Life for us in St. Louis was good, except for the lingering evils of racism and poverty we could not overlook. St. Louis also provided a good place to recover from my loss of a tremendously rich theological life in Tübingen. The theological consortium in St. Louis included the great Lutheran seminary, Concordia, and the Jesuit community at St. Louis University. As I learned, the Catholics and Lutherans know how to do theology with the amenities of good food and drink that make us poorer Protestants a little antsy. We became lifelong fans of the St. Louis Cardinals, even when they faltered at the last minute in the World Series.

One major ecumenical endeavor I undertook while at Eden was the Oxford Institute of Methodist Theological Studies, which is the only international body of Methodist theological scholars from all strands of Methodism stemming from the original Wesleyan movement, including the African Methodist Episcopal, African Methodist Episcopal Zion, and Christian Methodist Episcopal churches. Beginning in 1982, I served as co-chair of the Institute for twenty-five years. Blair and I were so often in Oxford and London that we began to know those cities better than the ones where we lived in this country.

In the summer of 1990, I became Dean and Professor of Systematic Theology at Wesley Theological Seminary at American University in Washington, DC. The campus is located near Ambassador Row on Massachusetts Avenue. The real estate surrounding it was so expensive that faculty had to live some distance from the campus. We had landed in our favorite city, Washington, DC, a short train trip to Philadelphia, New York City, and Boston. We had an East Coast consciousness from our literary past, but now it was more concrete. Not far from our house in DC was a nearly unrecognizable earthwork Civil War fortification, on the perimeter defenses of the city. I became more interested in the history of the Civil War with major battlefields just down the road. Prominent was Antietam, the bloodiest battle up to that time in modern warfare because of the introduction of repeating rifles. The trenches had been piled high with bodies, a sight that became familiar in the frequent subsequent wars to which we Americans sent our sons and daughters.

The 1990s was a decade of secularization and globalization, and their implications occupied the mind of the Wesley faculty. Secularization seemed to be a major crisis for denominations that had been declining in membership since the 1970s. Churches, synagogues, and mosques were shrinking except for a few megachurches and the extreme right evangelical movement. As for globalization, there is still no agreement on whether it is good or bad in our politics or other parts of society. For some, globalization means importing other cultures from around the world to dilute degrading aspects of American culture. For other Americans, as for many people around the world, globalization crushes their livelihood and neighborhood.

In the fall of 1998, I returned to Vanderbilt as faculty. The campus looked the same, but much had changed. The faculty and students were much more diverse. People of color were in administrative roles. The university had assumed a sense that its future lay in the future of the state, the nation, and the world. It was a good place to be and felt like home. In many ways I was actually returning home, closer to family and to the old haunts of Memphis I had earlier escaped. The chair I occupied had responsibility for teaching systematic theology and also developing relationships with the church. In connection with the latter responsibility, I was often in Memphis and traveled for lectures to many colleges and universities in the Southeast.

Vanderbilt was founded in 1875 by Holland McTyeire, a Methodist bishop who wanted to establish a great university for the South that could help heal the wounds of the Civil War. McTyeire 's wife was a relative of the wife of Cornelius Vanderbilt, who had been persuaded by McTyeire to give a vast amount of money to establish the university. The school was named for the donor instead of the one who had the vision and did the work. In 1914, some reactionary leaders of the Methodist Church South had caused a split with Vanderbilt because they viewed it as too progressive. Despite this separation, the Divinity School remained related to the Methodist Church. And during my time on the faculty, the relationship flourished. There were now funds for attracting excellent students and situating them in internships in churches.

As I continue my research and writing, I often look back to the Central days, especially my senior year, and the riveting insight for me that slavery is the problem not just of the American South, but of the human race altogether. Aristotle, arguably the most influential philosopher in the West, was profoundly wrong in one horrendous decision he made. In his *Republic* he held that some humans are less than human and therefore fit to be nothing but slaves. In many different ways this conviction appears in Western society through today. It was not his original idea. It was an idea created over many generations of plundering resources and enslaving kidnapped people for profit. The cancer of Western civilization is the assumption that enslavement of some is necessary for the liberty of others. We still live under the lame assumption that the end of chattel slavery in American law was the end of all the legacies of that sort of enslavement. The sins of the fathers are not our sins, but our failure to deal with the consequences of their sins, are our sins.

Despite the fact that Israel and the early church were surrounded by slavery, as was the whole of antiquity, and despite the fact that slavery appears in the Bible, I believe that the Bible is an antislavery book. The story of Jews and Christians begins, as it does today, at the Seder with the words, "Once we were slaves." Liberation is the primary story of exodus in the Hebrew scriptures. In our time, it is urgent to see all the dimensions of slavery: economic, political, cultural, natural, and spiritual. We are best off when we are shocked again and again by what the Bible, and the best of the world's novels and poetry make clear: The master is enslaved by his mastery of others. In *Moby Dick,* Ishmael asks, "Who ain't a slave? Tell me that."

As I return often in my imagination to Memphis, I remember its beauty: the quiet, steady flow of the Mississippi, the unequaled majesty of Memphis trees swaying in the breeze and the azaleas blazing in color in April, the voice of Marguerite Piazza that caused me to fall in love with opera, the gospel depth of Elvis and Johnny Cash that stuns with every hearing, and the long afternoons of unbounded childhood play on Graham Street. But this is not sweet nostalgia because it is remembering a past that was not good for others: those who were not at the table, not on the team, not in elected offices, not recognized, those who were in other schools, separated but not equal, those who were bent down by redlining, unreliable or no insurance, absence from employment lists, no forgiven debt, the lack of name in public, no representative in places of power, and fear of police.

The future of the church and of society depends on how we come to grips with the legacy of enslavement, including poverty. Race, inequality, classism, gender issues, the degradation of nature, our fearing other world religions and ideologies, and the possibility of nuclear destruction -- all these ways of taking down humanity are real threats. It is difficult to see how all these threats are interrelated and how complicated it is to come up with a human repair (*tikkun olam* in Hebrew) of our common life.

I devoted my life to the university with the conviction that education can enhance the life of every person and every community. But I have become keenly aware that the university is one of the chief causes of inequality as well. Repair is very difficult. The repair of ourselves is the most difficult. We Americans have long believed that the best common means of governing is democracy, but we have recently fallen out of agreement and have come close to losing democracy. To stay in hope is hard. For those of us who are still trying, our task is to leave to our grandchildren a hope that could empower them to carry on the struggle.

I don't have much to leave except the Bible's vision of God's redemption and an ounce of courage to stand up for it. In a secular society with little memory, this vision appears unrealistic. It is, however, the most realistic thing I know, because without it we have no long-range future. So, I treasure glimpses of the races living together, the poor and the rich finding a common love not measured by anything but self-giving -- new life with no new hierarchies, no redlining, no forgiving of debt for corporations but not for the poor, each of us protecting the vote of all. It is a vision in which reconciliation changes everyone and values everyone in a new way. Through the years, I have continued to see that in order to hope for this future of life, the best thing we can do is to live with and, by the grace of God, to love the vulnerable. For surely, God hears their cries and prayers first.

Doug Meeks, 2020

Doug and Blair Meeks, 2019

3 - Charlotte Dreve Clark

1962 - James Meredith integrates Ole Miss

In the week leading up to September 30, 1962, several of my sorority sisters and I played our regular card games of bridge in one of the bedrooms of our sorority house on the Ole Miss campus. The juniors and seniors who lived in the Kappa Kappa Gamma house often played cards between or after classes. But during that week, there was none of the music on the radio dial that usually accompanied our games. Instead, it was replaced by nonstop news, because something big was about to happen on our campus at University of Mississippi.

I remember that day in particular, hearing the reporter announce that a cavalcade of cars was leaving Memphis and bringing James Meredith, a Black man, to enroll at the university at Oxford -- the first Black person ever to attend our all-white university. If the governor of Mississippi, Ross Barnett, refused to admit him, all our degrees would be worthless, because the University of Mississippi would lose its accreditation. This same information had been broadcast several times that week, but no caravan had materialized. The thought of racial integration was not so much a fear to me, but the idea of having to start my education anew was a devastating thought. However, to many of my classmates, integration was unthinkable.

I grew up in a segregated Memphis. I had seen the water fountains with "white" and "colored" written above them. I had attended all-white elementary, junior high, and high schools. Living in the Bethel Grove area of town, I rode a city bus to both Fairview Junior High and Central High and knew that Black people had to ride in the back of the bus. My mother worked, and I had been cared for by Black women -- Magdelene, Florida, or Carrie -- who also cleaned our house. I always called them by their first name. And each would say, "Yes, ma'am" to me, even though I was a child, because that was "her place." Still, I said, "Yes, ma'am" to them too, because I was taught to say that to my elders. I was aware that they were supposed to ride in the back seat when they rode in our car. But I also knew Mother or Daddy would often tell them just to ride up front when we took them home.

In high school, I loved the shows at Ellis Auditorium downtown, featuring Black artists like Chuck Berry, Laverne Baker, and others. But I was aware that Black audience members had to sit in the balcony while the white audience sat downstairs. And, of course, I saw there were white and "Negro" neighborhoods. As a student at Memphis Central High, I had heard of the happenings at Little Rock Central High in 1957.

Still, in my memory, I lived an idyllic childhood. I played outdoors until dark at a time when doors were often left unlocked. Community centers, the Fairgrounds, and some churches provided us places to dance. I was a student before the drug craze. Unmarried pregnancies were few or unmentioned. I lived through segregation, but I was uninformed about the inequity of it, until I got to college.

I entered Ole Miss the second semester of my freshman year, after transferring from Mississippi State College for Women. At Ole Miss, I rushed and pledged Kappa Kappa Gamma and was honored to be elected president for my senior year. That's the reason I was the one who personally received a call from the sorority national headquarters with explicit instructions for the upcoming weekend that September in 1962. Ole Miss would be playing Kentucky on Saturday night. Suspecting possible trouble, headquarters told me to call a meeting of the girls and to tell them, if they intended to go to the game, to stay away from the governor's home and to behave in a proper manner. The organizers of an anti-integration protest were calling for people to form a human chain around the governor's mansion on Sunday to prevent Governor Barnett from letting Meredith enroll.

As we drove to Jackson, the capital of Mississippi, for the ballgame that Saturday, the radio stations blared "Go Mississippi, Keep Rolling Along," "Dixie," and similar songs to inspire us to prepare to fight for what many believed was a threatened way of life. The game was played, and we stayed the night. We made a quick drive by the vicinity of the Governor's mansion early in the day and saw several people already gathering to form their human chain. However, we returned to a quiet campus in Oxford, as we did most Sunday afternoons. The difference was that while all was seemingly happening in Jackson, Ross Barnett had already met and enrolled James Meredith on campus. Mr. Meredith was officially a student without anyone knowing it yet.

Our sorority house was in the process of building an addition, so there were bricks around the site. After dark on that night of September 30, we heard voices and looked out the window to see people coming from outside our campus, picking up bricks from our construction site and moving toward the Grove, in the center of campus. We heard noises later coming from there, but we were getting all our information from the radio or from hearsay. We went to bed not fully aware of what exactly was going on that evening. The next morning, my 8 a.m. English grammar class was canceled. As I walked across campus to attend my Monday 1 p.m. Victorian literature class, I found out it had also been canceled. A haze of smoke permeated the air. I assumed it was tear gas remaining from the night before, during what came to be known as "The Battle of Oxford." Two people were killed and several hundred, I believe, injured. In that week, I had to cast aside my childhood naiveté and make some grown-up decisions.

White parents, fearful for their child's safety, began fetching their students from campus and searching for a new place to send their kids to college. My father, at the urging of my mother, kept calling to tell me he was coming for me. I insisted that I was not leaving and that he could not come on campus because National Guardsmen were posted at each entrance to the university grounds to turn away anyone who did not belong. I felt that my place was to remain there and be a role model for those who had stayed and to be a help to the housemother as she tried to achieve some sort of normalcy. After repeated pleas, my parents finally trusted my actions. Several students returned to Ole Miss after a brief absence, but many did enroll elsewhere.

A sorority sister of mine was the editor of the college newspaper. She was a Memphis girl, a product of East High. Sidna Brower wrote an editorial the night Meredith enrolled, and at other times afterward, including when Meredith's dorm room was trashed. Sidna said, in essence, that all people, regardless of their skin color, were entitled to an education without fear of harm to their bodies or possessions. She was censured by the Campus Senate for her viewpoint. One night, I received word that a group of Kappa Alpha fraternity members were coming to our Kappa Kappa Gamma house to insist that we rescind her membership in the sorority. I knew without hesitation my response, but I did not have a right to speak for the others. I called a meeting that night in the living room and informed the girls that I was not going to agree to meet the guys' demands, and if they wanted to elect a new president, they could. The dissenters -- there were some in the house who were of like mind with the Kappa Alphas -- remained silent. No one spoke. So, I continued as president. And I took my scared self out onto the porch.

My nervousness that night is probably responsible for my not remembering all the facts. I know that I was not alone, but I don't recall who accompanied me -- probably our housemother and another member whose opinion aligned with mine. We stood on the porch, and the KAs stood one step down on the sidewalk, facing us, like opposing armies on a battlefield. I said that we would not be meeting their demands that night or any other. Thus, Sidna remained a Kappa and survived living in a house with a number of hostile sorority sisters. She was nominated for a Pulitzer Prize for her work at the student paper and appeared in several national newspaper articles and on some television programs.

She never met James Meredith while she was in Oxford. It wouldn't be until forty years later, at the 2003 anniversary commemoration of that night, that she and he finally spoke. Former members of the Campus Senate, who were also at the event that night, claimed that they had not participated in their censure of Sidna. It is interesting to see how the tides that shunned Sidna back then had changed, and they felt compelled to deny their roles in her rebuke at the time.

I never saw Meredith when I was a student either. I saw his body-guards, and I heard about his being on campus, but basically life went on as before. For quite a while, whenever we would enter or exit the campus, a National Guardsman would order us to "dismount the vehicle." Then one would search our trunk and our glove compartment. There were several young and attractive guardsmen, so we would try to think of embarrassing items to put in the areas to be searched.

That was the extent of our experience of the aftermath of what was called desegregation. I continued my education by student teaching in Meridian, Mississippi, and earned my valid degree in May of 1963. In the fall of 1963, I began my teaching career back in Memphis and taught for four years at Treadwell Junior High. In addition, I taught summer school for three summers at East High.

For more than fifty years, I have taught as either a lead teacher or a substitute teacher in Memphis, St. Louis, North Little Rock, and southeast Missouri. I consistently taught English throughout that time -- including classes in Shakespeare, mythology, novels, and ACT prep -- although I was coerced into teaching a class in geography and two classes of physical education during my early years. I sponsored the Beta Club, Scholar Bowl, cheerleaders, and student council and helped decorate for proms. I stocked soda machines, sold Little Debbies, candy, brass, wrapping paper, pizzas, magazines, and more -- anything to make money to help pay for our many trips and expenses. I have graded essays and research papers on many a Sunday afternoon and have critiqued papers for many students who sought my help. I love my students. That has been one constant over the years. The kids at all my schools have been, for the most part, great.

I remember one day during my first semester of teaching in 1963, I was walking from the senior high building back to my classroom in the junior high at Treadwell when a student came toward me in some distress and said, "The president has been shot!" I thought, "The president of the student council? Or the president of the United States?" Neither was a palatable option. It was the assassination of John F. Kennedy. School was dismissed, and we all watched the replay and the aftermath on the television at home.

In 1967, I married my fiancé, Ken, and I left Treadwell to teach in St. Louis, where he had a job. The senseless death of our young president was not the end of the violence of that time. In spring of 1968, Martin Luther King, Jr. was assassinated on the balcony of the Lorraine Motel in my hometown of Memphis, as he joined a protest of Black sanitation workers on strike to improve wages and working conditions. A mere two months later, Senator Robert Kennedy was killed at a campaign rally.

Ken was transferred to Memphis in the fall of 1968, and I was fortunate to be reassigned to Treadwell upon our return. When I discovered that I was expecting our first child, I was told I would have to quit in December because there was a rule that teachers could not teach after the fourth or fifth month of pregnancy. Fortunately, someone with good sense allowed me to stay until the end of semester in mid-January. Otherwise, the students would have had a stranger review and give them their final exam. Our son Chris was born in May of 1970, and I prepared to return to Treadwell. But because I had lost my tenure when I married and moved, I was reassigned.

In 1970, the Memphis City Schools decided to set the wheels of school busing in motion, which caused a number of white religious leaders, likewise, to set in motion a plan to open a number of Christian academies to avoid integration. White families started the exodus from the city, east to the suburbs. The city school system determined that integrating the faculties before integrating the students was the wisest plan. That is how I became one of the 40 percent of white faculty members assigned to a school with an all-Black student body -- in my case it was Lester Junior High.

I was once again involved in trying to do my tiny part to make education equal for all. The experience at Lester was more favorable than not. The students were most receptive. They were no different from students anywhere. If I was more of an oddity, they didn't show their curiosity. We joined hands and sang, "We Shall Overcome" during a pep assembly. A group huddled for a picture. One student encouraged me to pose in the center of the photo "to lighten it up." I obliged. It was not said with disrespect or sarcasm. Most of the teachers were kind and helpful, and a few became dear friends with whom I kept in contact until health issues or distance intervened. My family left Memphis, as we had and would with other moves, because of my husband's job. He began working with Falstaff Brewing Company as their sales representative in Arkansas in 1971.

During our five years in North Little Rock, we welcomed our second son, Cory. I was hired to teach at a school with 1,500 seventh graders. During that time, an attempt was made to assassinate Alabama governor George Wallace in Alabama. In the 1960s and 1970s, our society had to acclimate itself to violence, and I had to help the students understand what was going on.

On the positive side, the Women's movement in the 1970s had a constructive impact on teachers, who were mostly women. Shortly after I left Memphis, federal courts ruled that to prevent a pregnant woman from teaching was sex discrimination. One of my coworkers in Arkansas had challenged the rule. By then, we could also wear slacks in the classroom. Teachers pay was improving too but had a long way to go. I remember being excited when my pay in St. Louis in 1968 increased to $3,700 a year, the same amount as the cost of our new car.

Falstaff changed ownership and decided to eliminate the salesmen from the merchandising equation. Thus, Ken accepted a position with Bluff City Beer Company, a beer distributorship, which at that time had five warehouses in southeast Missouri. So, we relocated to Kennett, Missouri, and I went from teaching seventh through tenth graders to teaching exclusively high schoolers in Steele, Missouri. I can still feel the fear I felt when I was told I would teach senior English. And along with the older students came the responsibility of sponsoring proms and clubs, for which we got no extra pay. I taught English to all three grades for three years straight, from 1976 to 1979, and sponsored the senior prom too. Those students who had me all three years at South Pemiscot High School maintained a relationship with me for several years. They even invited Ken and me to several of their reunions. I felt like maybe they thought I was a member of their class.

In 1979, Ken was transferred to Poplar Bluff, Missouri, his hometown. That is when all our moving around stopped. In fact, I still live in Poplar Bluff today. I was hired to teach at a school called Twin Rivers, in the nearby small town of Broseley, Missouri.

Along with changes for students, many aspects of being a teacher have changed since I started in 1963. One of the major differences was the dress code. At Ole Miss, my wardrobe consisted primarily of dresses, and skirts and tops. An accessory at the time was a single strand of pearls. Pants were not the norm, but a new fashion, the mini skirt, was a necessity for each wardrobe. Whenever I headed to Sardis Dam to sun or swim, a skirt -- preferably a wrap-around -- had to be worn over the shorts or bathing suit on campus, even if I was just going to the car. Teachers in Memphis had a dress code, too. We had to wear dresses. Slacks were not allowed until later. I wore high heels most of the time. I even had to don a wrap-around skirt one year when I taught a physical education class between English classes. These rules are archaic now. But they didn't seem so bad then, since we had heard stories of teachers prior to our generation not being allowed to wear patent leather shoes, as the gloss would reflect, and the boys could see up women's dresses. Also, before us, teachers could not even marry.

Naturally, I have seen changes in technology in education through the years too. Before I graduated from college, I took a class in audio-visual equipment. I learned how to use a film projector. The need was short-lived, as we progressed to VCRs with VHS tapes and then to CDs and DVRs. When I first taught, I recorded grades on report cards. Then I had grade sheets and sent them to the office. The year before I retired in May of 2000, we had workshops on how to put grades onto a computer. Now, everything is done on computers. What little knowledge I have about computers, I gained when I took that workshop. I am still barely computer literate.

After I retired, I rested for a year. But then, I began substitute teaching, which I still do, even in my eighties. These days, I am surrounded by a faculty largely comprising my former students. I feel a great sense of pride that some of these wonderful teachers may have chosen to teach because of something I said or had them do for me.

When I was at Central, I had that same experience. In fact, Central High was instrumental in my career decision. I was in Coach Malcolm Phillips' class the first year. He rarely stayed in class because he had to take care of basketball business. Thus, he left me in charge, and usually with numerous papers to grade. The fact that he was one of my favorite teachers and that he trusted me to help him was instrumental in solidifying the kernel of desire that I already had to be a teacher.

However, my favorite of favorite teachers had to be Miss Cornelia Crinkley, a math teacher, who was chock-full of sarcastic comments. I was horrid in math. I took Algebra from her. Then, two years later, it was a credit to her teaching style that I definitely wanted her class when I had to take Algebra II. I had had an abominable time in Geometry the prior year. I needed redeeming. Evidently, I had matured because I made A's and B's in her class that year. I remember that we had to take a bus downtown on Saturdays or holidays to research mathematicians. She always gave us a grade on some kind of research work each grading period, so we would have one test grade based on creativity or organization. And I was very good at coloring and organizing. I implemented her idea in many of my English classes when I taught, by assigning an art project, a memory passage, or a reenactment of a scene to go along with different works of literature.

For the last forty years, from my last two decades as a full-time teacher to my two decades of substitute teaching, I have been in the same school of 300 or fewer students in four grades in rural Missouri. In the early years I was there, students who were gay hid their sexuality, remaining in the closet. Today, some of my favorite kids are openly gay or lesbian. And although I may not know everything that goes on, for the most part, I do not detect any of the bullying that occurred in the past, only acceptance, or at least tolerance.

My beloved husband Ken died in 2020. Our son Chris lives with me in Missouri and works at a wellness center. Our younger son Cory is retired from a twenty-six-year career in the military -- twenty-four years of which he served as a Navy SEAL. He and his wife live in Virginia, and my three granddaughters and three great-grands reside on the Mississippi Gulf Coast.

I believe throughout my life, the structure, values, and education I received from my parents and in college during a tumultuous time taught me to accept change and be comfortable with it. When I was choosing a career in the early 1960s, women did not have too many acceptable options.

You could be a secretary, nurse, homemaker, or teacher. Even if I had had more options, though, I do not think I would have chosen any other profession. I think that is the reason that I still substitute several days a week at the last school where I taught full time. And I firmly believe that all my teachers at Central and elsewhere prepared me to be the best that I could be at the only occupation I ever wanted.

Charlotte Dreve Clark and Ken Clark, London, 1999   Charlotte Dreve Clark, 2020

4 - Cathy Cade

1963 - The Albany, Georgia Voting Rights Campaign

Two weeks after my June 1963 graduation from Carleton College in Minnesota, I ended up in Albany, Georgia, working with civil rights activists on voting rights campaigns and efforts to desegregate public places. On my second day in Albany, I was going through a Black neighborhood knocking on doors and asking people to attend a mass meeting organized by the Student Nonviolent Coordinating Committee (SNCC). It was one of the first times that SNCC put Black and white volunteers together, doing this kind of field work in the South. It was right where I wanted to be.

But not long into our work that day, I saw the police taking my two companions into custody. I went over, showed my identification, and asked what was happening. The police officer told me he was arresting my colleagues for loitering and vagrancy. Then, seeing I was working with them, he said I was under arrest too. So, I sat down on the ground in protest, as I had been taught to do in our nonviolence direct action trainings. Immediately, two patrolmen picked me up, tugged me along the ground, put me in the back of a patrol car and took me to the city jail. When I asked them why they thought I was doing something wrong, they told me any white girl in shorts, a sleeveless sweater, and open-toed shoes, walking around the streets in an all-Black section of town was considered suspicious.

Once we got to jail, there were seven of us in an eight-by-eight-foot cell meant for four people. There were four beds and a mattress on the floor, and a sink and a toilet. We could tell when an officer was approaching by the jingle of keys hanging from his belt. The jail was segregated, of course, so there were four sections in the jail: Black male, Black female, white male, and white female. Some older Black men who were in jail but were not part of the movement were made to do janitorial work. They would sometimes carry notes back and forth between these sections. For nine days we never left our cells, except for one interview with the police. We spent our days talking, reading, and sleeping. Paperback books were sent to us from up North, and because there were so few books, we tore them into parts and circulated them so that everyone could have a piece to read. It was cool in the mornings, so we needed blankets. But then it was hot in the day.

In a letter I wrote to my parents from jail, I said, "My purpose here is to try and assist demonstrations to the end of achieving some meaningful desegregation. You say things are getting out of hand, and to a degree this is true. That is why SNCC (pronounced "snick") is even more important than ever, for the people are tired, and they are beginning to know that things do not have to be the way they are. If this frustration and anger is not organized and channeled, even more violence will occur with no beneficial results for the Negro community. You begin to realize that this fight is not something you pick up after you have done your homework, but something affecting the whole way of life of thousands of people. Things are changing, but so far, they have made little difference in the everyday life of most Negroes. Children are still growing up knowing there are vast numbers of experiences never open to them just because they are Negroes."

As the days progressed, I was feeling stronger and stronger. I was beginning to understand where I was, with whom, and why. Also, I was being liberated from the lie that going to jail meant your life was over. I had never felt so alive.

Early on during our time in jail, we decided to go on a hunger strike, to draw more national attention to the situation in Albany. Besides, the food looked awful, and we only had to resist eating three times a day. We sang together and said grace together as a group, before we returned our food uneaten. As the days went by, I began to spend long periods of time fantasizing about food. In the end, my favorite fantasy was about hard-boiled eggs and tomato soup. Our hunger, lack of space, and lack of exercise began to wear on us as a group. We would be talking about something and suddenly someone would be talking about food. This was the situation when Albany's chief of police came into our cell eating a piece of lemon meringue pie. He "offered" us some. It was a cruel trick. But no one gave in.

When it came time for our court dates, we could hardly walk up the stairs. Our legs were truly weak from lying on our bunks for nine days. We had on the same clothes from the day we were arrested. At trial, a young Black lawyer represented us, telling the court the police had harassed SNCC by picking up the organizers, and by following them. He also mentioned that the police had referred to the white girls in SNCC using the n-word with the word "bleached" before it. He moved for dismissal based on no probable cause for our arrests. The motion was overruled. However, we received a suspended sentence and were free to go, with the stipulation that we would leave town and go home.

Because my father was concerned about my arrest, he came to Albany to rescue me, and to see for himself what was going on. I never wanted my father to come. In fact, I was furious and embarrassed that he was there. I could not believe he was talking to and trusting the white authorities, and that he was talking with the leading white segregationist lawyers in town. In retrospect, I see that that trip to Albany added to the stress that led to his brief nervous breakdown when we returned to Chicago. My mother wrote me that what worried my father as much as my physical safety was that he was sure I was becoming a Communist. I was his oldest child, and he was scared about my life. I was young and idealistic. He was a rabid Republican.

Back in Chicago, I was angry at my father for tricking me into coming home, and for making the racist assumption that Negroes could only be fighting for their freedom if they were duped. I was infuriated with him for interfering in my life. But I could also see that he was very scared, and I felt I owed him something for raising me. I went home for two weeks (had some tomato soup and hard-boiled eggs) and then as a compromise with my father's fear, and not without some of my own, I decided to spend the rest of the summer in SNCC Atlanta headquarters, doing office work.

My family moved from the Chicago suburbs to Memphis in 1955, when my father was given a new assignment at International Harvester. I was fourteen at the time and the eldest of five children in an upper-middle-class family. I was in constant and fierce competition with my oldest brother. I was taught that everyone is equal, and that you can be special if you work hard and get ahead. I was expected to achieve in school, and I did.

I grew up different from the other children in the Midwestern and Southern neighborhoods where we lived. I was often treated as a newcomer, because our family moved so often for my father's work. We were Unitarians, not a very well-known religion outside the Northeast at the time. I was marginal, but not isolated, because I had my mother's support and that of the church. My childhood experience made it easier for me to be "different" as an adult. I didn't recognize the possibility of being a lesbian until my late twenties, when I became a part of the Women's Movement of the 1960s and 1970s.

Among other projects, my father was part of a team of engineers designing better mechanical cotton pickers. These cotton pickers were displacing the Black labor force in the nearby Mississippi Delta region -- a major economic and political change in the area. My father was central to my life. I grew up hating him for being unfair, mean, and scary. He had a lot of rage. But I also loved and respected him, and I never stopped trying to understand him. I respected his commitment to learning and hard work. I loved the stories he brought to the dinner table of how he got around the irrationality and ineptness of the large bureaucracies where he worked -- the U.S. Army, John Deere, and International Harvester. Finally, he taught me to laugh big.

At the all-white Central High School in Memphis, I was active in intramurals and several clubs, including speech and science. I first heard of the civil rights movement when I was in the ninth grade and someone in the Unitarian Church told me about Martin Luther King, Jr. and the bus boycott in Montgomery, Alabama. The Memphis Unitarian Church happened to be across the street from Central. I found support there for my integrationist ideas, which started young and have continued throughout my life.

During our time in Memphis, I have wonderful memories of Mary Brown. She was the Black woman who worked for our family. Mary first arrived at our house to help unpack our moving van in her job with a local moving company, and she proceeded to ask my mother for a job as a house-keeper. She was not a big woman, but she had a big scar across her cheek. My mother respected Mary for her leadership of her multigenerational family. When we first lived in Memphis, my mother told me that Mary's mother was the matriarch, and Mary was next in line. When her mother died, Mary became the head of their family and sent her daughter, Rhea, to work at our house. Mary would take my younger sister and brothers to her house to play, but I did not get to go because, at fifteen, I was considered too old. It was not uncommon in the South for Black and white children to play together until they got to a certain age, nearing sexual maturity, and then white people forbade those friendships. When Rhea's son, Preacher, would come by our house with his mother, I would try and talk with him, but he would move from room to room and leave very quickly, looking very uncomfortable or even scared. Our church youth group had two meetings with Black youth from a nearby Black Baptist church. This was my only connection with young Black people while I lived in Memphis.

During my junior year in high school, Central High School in Little Rock, Arkansas was integrated, under the watch of the National Guard. I remember one day when I was in one of my classes, the teacher asked the class what we thought about what was going on at Little Rock Central. I was the only one who spoke up, saying I was for racial integration. I do not think the teacher liked my answer, because she looked like she was going to faint. Not knowing how to respond back to the class, or to me, she quickly changed the subject. At Central High, many students repeated the awful cheer of that time: "Two-four-six-eight, we don't want to integrate."

When I graduated from high school, I chose a liberal arts college in Minnesota, Carleton College. Less than a year later, my father was promoted again, and the family moved to Hinsdale, Illinois, a wealthy suburb of Chicago. In the spring of 1962, my junior year of college, I participated in an exchange program at Spelman College, a Black women's college in Atlanta. Deciding to apply for this program was my first decision independent of my parents. I wanted to go to Spelman because I was becoming more aware of racial issues and wanted the experience of going to an all-Black college.

When I told my parents, they were nervous, but they did not try to stop me. My parents were very pro-education, and my mother, at least, had raised me not to be prejudiced. There were seven white exchange students from seven different colleges at Spelman. The first week there, I took part in a demonstration led by Howard Zinn, the progressive historian and author of *A People's History of the United States*. We had a sit-in at the Negro section of the Georgia State Senate in Atlanta. We left before we were arrested. That semester, I took classes at Spelman and Morehouse Colleges, hanging out with my new friends at the SNCC office, taking part in more demonstrations, doing some voter registration work, and attending a SNCC conference.

My time at Spelman had a great and enriching influence on my life. I was becoming more conscious about human rights. I wanted to take steps away from my white, upper-middle-class upbringing. I saw the limits of what my racial and class background was teaching me about how you were supposed to be. I feel very lucky that I got to have that experience.

I tried to bring some of what I had learned at Spelman back to Carleton when I returned to finish my undergraduate degree. I arranged for the Freedom Singers to perform on campus. They were an a cappella quartet of Black students from Georgia who sang protest songs to raise money for SNCC. I brought Frank Smith to speak on campus. He was a student speaker who gave talks about the tyranny of segregation, to raise money for SNCC. And I worked with four churches and the two colleges in town to collect clothes and books to send to people living in poverty in Black communities of the Mississippi Delta. Those were some of the same people being denied the right to register to vote. Carleton students donated 120 boxes of clothes, and the University of Minnesota collected 4,000 pounds of food, which were all trucked to Mississippi, for free, by members of the Teamsters Union.

The next fall I started graduate school at Tulane University in New Orleans. I was there two days when I got a call that SNCC workers were in town to help with voter registration. For a couple of weeks, I joined them. During my first year at Tulane, I spent many weekends in Jackson, Mississippi planning for what came to be called Freedom Summer in 1964 -- a massive voter registration drive across the state. I was a leader in North Gulfport, Mississippi that summer, specializing in phone calls with the police about who had been recently arrested. They would ask, "Is this 'ole Cathy?"

I attended the founding conference of the Southern Student Organizing Committee in Nashville in May of 1964. The next year at Tulane,

I helped found and lead an organization called Students for Integration, which was a multi-campus student effort to desegregate restaurants in accordance with the newly passed Civil Rights Bill. In the summer of 1965, I worked with civil rights legend Matt Suarez in New Orleans' fourth ward. And I helped found and lead the Tulane Chapter of the Students for Democratic Society (SDS), which began to take on the issues of the Vietnam War.

In 1966 and 1967, I lived in Canton, Mississippi, where I did research for my dissertation on attitudes in the Black community about using consensus versus conflict methods of social change. By 1967, it was time to write my dissertation on what the Black community thought was the best way to bring social change. I found that working-class Black people believed in agitation and direct action, while Black people who were well-off or were living in poverty believed being law-abiding, educated, and working hard was the way to social change. I received my PhD in Sociology in 1969. Once back in New Orleans in 1969, I was part of the early Women's Liberation Movement, and we started a local women's consciousness raising group, which included several women who had been in the Civil Rights Movement in various parts of the South.

I moved to San Francisco in 1970, to be a part of the larger women's movement there. It was so much easier there to find and get together with women who were choosing the same things I wanted at that moment. I began to work full time in the women's movement. Very soon, I came out as a lesbian, and I became a photographer. I had seen the power of photography in 1962 in Atlanta while working at SNCC. Renowned photographers would use the office's photo lab, developing photos they published to gain support for the movement across the country, much like our cell phones do today. When the SNCC photographer, Bill Light, moved to San Francisco in 1971 he offered to teach me photography and lend me his darkroom.

In the mid-1970s, I decided I wanted to have a child by donor insemination, and I asked a gay friend to find me an anonymous donor so I could get pregnant. My gay friend brought me the sperm of another gay man, and in 1978, I gave birth to a son in San Francisco whom I named after the gay activist Carl Whittman. I had known Carl in the civil rights movement in New Orleans, where he participated in a children's playgroup that people in the women's movement had organized for our kids. I visited him once or twice in Oregon, where he lived near lesbian friends of mine. When I gave birth to my son, I labored at home with a lot of friends surrounding me, a lot of those lesbian neighbors. However, I ended up having to go to the hospital because I needed a C-section, and some of them came with me to provide support. My second son was born in 1985, also by donor insemination.

I had had some interactions with gay men and had no prejudices toward them. I was never a lesbian separatist, partly because I had been in the civil rights movement, and I had been so close to men, especially Black men in that movement.

Probably more than half of us had boys in our lesbian mothers' group. It was a big issue. The separatists did not want us to bring our young male children to the music festivals and to some other events, which I understood. But I believed that lesbian mothers had the power to raise sons who would respect women and treat them as equals. I believed that men did not have to be oppressive.

The 1980s were a time of working on my book of photographs and interviews, *A Lesbian Photo Album: The Lives of Seven Lesbian Feminists*, which was published in 1987. In the 1990s, I expanded my collection of photographs of lesbian mothering as I continued to raise my sons.

In 2000, I founded another business called, Cathy Cade: Personal Histories, Photo Organizing, and Photography. I helped my clients record and preserve their histories. I brought the skills, joys, and commitments of my experiences to my services and artistic work. Over the years, I have gradually healed from the complexity of my relationship with my parents and have reclaimed parts of my life that I thought I had to leave behind when I left the South.

In the first two decades of the twenty-first century, I began documenting the history of the Bay Area women's movement and the Bay Area's lesbian community -- from California's earliest Pride parades to women working as mechanics to the 2011 Occupy movement. I supported myself by teaching college, being on welfare, housecleaning, doing office work, teaching photography in high school, and administering a project that helped people in developing countries build wheelchairs. In 2012, UC-Berkeley's Bancroft Library acquired my full photo archive. It is the library's only full archive from a lesbian photographer, and I hope the photos will help future generations understand where we were, and what we did.

I am proud of what we in the movement were able to do in the face of opposition. Each of my family members has been proud of my work, which also significantly influenced their lives. Three of my five siblings live in interracial households and have raised mixed-race children. Another brother was active in a mentoring program for inner-city youth in Chicago, and another brother was part of a land co-op in Costa Rica. For many years, my mother supported racial justice issues through the Unitarian Church. My siblings and I benefited from my mother's progressive values. I would hate to see my civil rights work and the efforts of the rest of my family discounted as merely a rebellion against our father. However, I believe that my siblings and I first directly experienced oppression as children at the hands of our father, which helped us identify with other oppressed groups.

But even my father changed more than I ever imagined a human being could change. After his bypass surgery, his emotional heart was often quite open. Driving past an underused Army base, he suggested it be made into housing for the homeless. He made special efforts to talk with and understand the unconventional lives of his five grown children. He gave me money so that I only needed a part-time job while I worked on my photography book about lesbian mothering. In return for the financial support, I had to write him quarterly progress reports. Doing these reports turned out to be quite helpful to me in understanding what I was accomplishing. When I remember these changes in my father, I experience great hope for change in the whole world.

My life has been a natural progression from participation in my Unitarian young people's group, to working in the Civil Rights Movement, the Women's Movement, the Lesbian and Gay Movement, to being a socialist, lesbian mother, and photographer. Much of my photography is done alone, but it directly expresses my political consciousness. My deepest wish is to find more ways to work for social change until the end of my life.

Cathy Cade

Gay Is Good, 1971, San Francisco, photo by Cathy Cade
© *The Regents of the University of California, The Bancroft Library,*
University of California, Berkeley

5 - Jerry Manley

1966 - The Vietnam War

Mayday. Mayday.

It was warm. No, it was hot. It was another routine day in Rach Gia, the province capital of South Vietnam's southernmost district on the shores of the Gulf of Thailand. I was a Lieutenant Junior Grade Navy Officer, serving as an advisor to the South Vietnamese Navy Coastal Division 45. Every American military member who served in Vietnam was called an advisor, to imply we weren't in active combat. But we were.

Mayday. Mayday.

It was Valentine's Day, 1966. I had flown from Saigon to Rach Gia on a U.S. Army aircraft eight days earlier. I was manning the operations watch that day, monitoring the radio for calls from any of our patrolling units -- U.S. Coast Guard large cutters, U.S. Navy Patrol Craft Fast boats, or PCFs, also known as "swift boats," and three South Vietnamese Coastal Craft Divisions.

Mayday. Mayday.

Mayday is the radio distress signal used by ships and aircraft. I had been trying to establish two-way communications with one of our swift boats ever since the first alert had sounded a few minutes before. Finally, the communication came through and it was alarming. "This is PCF 4 and we are sinking." And the next communication was heartbreaking. "We have casualties." I was able to locate their position, and as luck would have it, backup forces were nearby and could arrive quickly. But there was no luck in time to save the four swift boat crew members who died that day. Two sailors survived.

PCF 4 had been on its normal duty for many hours. As they did on any other day, the men were patrolling, boarding, searching, and patrolling again, scanning the blue waters and green shorelines. Their mission was to interdict and stop the flow of North Vietnamese troops, war materiel, and supplies into South Vietnam, by sea, land, and rivers. In the late afternoon, PCF 4 was patrolling offshore in Rach Gia Bay, on the northern side of the bay, not too distant from Rach Gia proper. At a little past 4 p.m., a crew-man spotted an object in the water close to the shore. They maneuvered their boat closer to the object. It was a small bamboo raft that was empty, except for a pole from which flew a Viet Cong flag. Viet Cong was the name given to South Vietnamese people who supported the North Vietnamese communist cause, and thusly the North Vietnam government. Our men came alongside to "capture" the souvenir, only to have an observer hidden in the tree line on the beach touch two wires together causing an explosion beneath PCF 4, ripping into her underbelly. She sank. PCF 4 was eventually recovered but was not usable.

The names of those four fallen sailors, and the 58,268 other service men and women who died in that war, are etched on the walls of the Vietnam Veterans Memorial in Washington, DC. They were young people who had not been able to reach their prime years. I have always remembered that day and those four sailors.

When not on patrol, I lived in a house in Rach Gia with other American military, and with civilian advisors (CIA agents). The American presence included all the branches of the military except Marine Corps personnel. We occupied two large houses next door to each other. Between the two houses there were about thirty Americans. But we didn't have much in the way of protection from the Viet Cong, or VC, who were plentiful in the region. It seems that an "understanding" existed between the local South Vietnamese Army Commander and the local VC forces, because the local VC used Rach Gia as a rest and relaxation center. So, despite the PFC 4 explosion, the town of Rach Gia was generally considered "safe." Once, when a new American senior Army advisor arrived for duty shortly after my arrival, he convinced his Vietnamese counterpart that security was too lax. That meant check points were then established entering town, with the expectation that more measures would be implemented. Within a week, limited rounds of mortar fire were directed toward the American compound as they never had been before. No building was damaged, and no personnel were injured. Pretty soon, the "understanding" was back in place. The check points were removed, and the mortar fire ceased, much to our relief.

During my time with Coastal Division 45:

A. We engaged the nearby VC in several actions, generally in conjunction with the patrolling swift boats.

B. I learned that operating with the CIA is not as much fun as it might sound.

C. Going to sea for ten days at a time, where seafood is the primary food staple and you are not a fan of fish, does not make you eagerly anticipate mealtime.

D. A quick and efficient way to "harvest" fish is to toss a concussion grenade into the water.

E.   The boats had no restrooms so you had to make do. One of my
fellow advisors was shot in the buttocks while making do.

It was a Thursday in October 1963 when my parents and my six-year-old sister drove me to the Memphis airport, and I flew to Norfolk, Virginia. Earlier that week, I had been coaching college football at Southwestern (now Rhodes College), when I was commissioned as an ensign in the U.S. Navy. Upon arrival in Virginia, I caught a cab to the bachelor officers' quarters at the Navy base. On Friday morning, I put on my civilian suit and tie, got directions, and proceeded to the office of the commander of amphibious force of the U.S. Atlantic Fleet. I had seen on a sign outside the building that the Admiral filling that position was named John McCain Jr. I entered the office and notified the Admiral's secretary that I was here to see Admiral McCain. I took a seat and shortly afterward was escorted into the Admiral's office. I was directed to a small table in the corner and the Admiral joined me. We talked for several minutes about the weather and other small talk.

Then, Admiral McCain asked me the purpose of my visit. I told him I'd been directed to report to him. He said he understood that, and I should go ahead and make my report. Confused, I said something to the effect that I was in town and ready to start my school. Admiral McCain looked at me for a while and then asked if I was a new ensign. I replied, "Yes, Sir." The Admiral started laughing, loudly. He must have noticed that I was uncomfortable and he stopped laughing, telling me not to be upset with his reaction. He said that a number of newly commissioned ensigns had attempted to report to him personally, but they had all been in uniform and his secretary had redirected them to the appropriate office. As I was dressed in a coat and tie, she had assumed I was a member of the Naval Investigative Service, which was the Navy's FBI, consisting of civilians. He then asked why I was not in uniform. I told him that on Monday I had been a football coach until I was commissioned as an ensign, and that I did not have any uniforms. The Admiral went to his desk and directed his aide to get Mr.

Thomas on the phone. Shortly thereafter, the Admiral was talking with the owner of Frank Thomas & Sons, a Navy uniform tailor shop in downtown Norfolk. The Admiral then summoned his driver, and I was driven to Mr. Thomas's store. When I reported for duty that next Monday to the Naval Amphibious School for my class, I was outfitted in a tailor-made Navy service blue uniform, delivered to me on Sunday by Mr. Thomas.

Upon completing various Navy schools, I assumed duties as the communications officer on the USS *Lindenwald*. I went to sea for the first time shortly after the beginning of 1964. It was certainly different from taking our family ski boat out for a spin back home. It is exciting to stand watch on the ship's bridge and feel the ship come alive decks below, under my feet, to start a new day. The cooks were up early baking bread and making the morning meal, followed shortly by the call for reveille, and the remaining crew members rolling out of their racks to prepare for the workday.

During our deployment in the Mediterranean later that summer, our ship was involved in a demonstration of our amphibious capabilities off the coast of one of the Greek islands. Part of the demonstration consisted of our Underwater Demolition Team (UDT) members jumping from a slow, low flying helicopter into the water and subsequently being retrieved by small craft, before proceeding to "targets" ashore. I was a backup radio operator on one of the helicopters that day. As part of the demonstration, my UDT buddies threw me out of the helicopter, to add an "accidental" element to the demonstration. And unlike the UDT members who were wearing khaki-colored swim trunks and blue tee shirts, I was dressed in my khaki uniform with long pants and a regular khaki shirt with buttons up the front. Eventually we made our way to the beach and were standing at attention as the two admirals there to inspect us made their way down the line. One was our commander, Admiral Ellis. The other was Admiral John McCain Jr., whom I had met months earlier when I showed up in his office by mistake. Admiral Ellis reached me, he shook my hand, chuckled, and commented that my scream of fright as I pretended to have fallen out of the aircraft sounded almost real. As Admiral McCain reached my position, he ran his eyes up and down my uniform, which was wet, wrinkled, and now missing several buttons. He winked and said Mr. Thomas would be disappointed at how I was treating his uniform. I was surprised he remembered me, but also pleased that he did.

I first arrived in Saigon on July 25, 1965. Our planeload of service personnel were ushered into a large conference room, where we were given a personal welcoming talk by General Westmoreland himself.

I had volunteered for duty in South Vietnam to serve as an advisor to the Vietnamese coastal force. At the conclusion of 1964, there had been 23,300 U.S. military personnel serving in South Vietnam. All these personnel were "advisors" to the government of South Vietnam under the command of General William Westmoreland. On March 8, 1965, the U.S. Marines landed the first intact unit of 3,500 personnel, to protect installations in the Da Nang area in the northern section of South Vietnam. By the end of 1965 there were 184,300 U.S. military deployed physically within South Vietnam. Of course, there were thousands more Navy and Air Force personnel supporting operations in the area.

During our training, we were not given particular units for our future assignments but were advised that those assignments would be made after our arrival in Saigon. Much to my disappointment during our arrival processing, I was informed that because of my previous Navy experience as a communications officer, I would not be assuming duties as an advisor to the Vietnamese Navy, but I would be redirected to the headquarters of the Naval Advisory Group (NAG) located in Saigon. A command and communication center was being constructed in the NAG headquarters. Disappointment aside, I went to work supporting the establishment of the new facility. After the communications center was up and running, I became a command center watch officer. Weekly, we rotated shifts, providing 24-hour coverage for the center. The assignment was rewarding and important, but living in Saigon, taking a taxi to work, and having dinner at a local hotel was not high on my interest list of military duty.

What did attract my interest was helping the children of Saigon, particularly those who resided at the Hoi Duc Anh orphanage. After seeing their circumstances, I got an idea of how I could be of use. I wrote a letter to the editor of the Memphis *Commercial Appeal* asking for support to assist with clothing for these girls and boys, which was published in late autumn of 1965. The response was difficult to believe. Several churches in Memphis took this plea as a Christmas challenge and responded in kind. Box after box arrived. I recruited others to help. In our off-duty time we would unpack, sort, repack, and deliver the items to the orphanage. It was absolutely amazing. Because of our final delivery on Christmas Eve, I missed the Bob Hope Christmas show at the air base.

Eventually, Rear Admiral Ward took a personal interest in finding a replacement so I could go out into the field and complete my tour in Vietnam as an advisor with the coastal force. I never knew exactly why he became involved. It might have been related to the orphanage effort. He most certainly was aware of it. He couldn't have missed the boxes stored in one of our unused rooms, and he had commented in a positive manner more than once. Or it might have been related to General Westmoreland and the red phone.

Behind our desks in the command center were a bank of phones. One of these phones was painted red. General Westmoreland's sleeping quarters were located in the same compound. When you removed the red phone from its cradle, it rang directly beside the general's bed, so we could alert him if there was a security threat to the compound. One night, when standing watch on the night shift, I absent-mindedly removed the red phone from its cradle, only to discover the general at the other end. And somehow I did that not just once, but three times. The first time, after listening to my apology, he laughed and hung up his phone. The second time, several weeks later after listening to my "Sorry, General," he asked my name. The third time, he answered by inquiring if this was Navy Lieutenant Manley. Then he hung up. I often wondered whether General Westmoreland suggested that Rear Admiral Ward help me find another assignment out of town. At any rate, that is when I was assigned to Rach Gia.

My life did not commence with my parents dropping me off at the airport for that flight to my first duty station in the Navy. No, I grew up in Memphis. We lived in East Memphis, near the intersection of Getwell and Park Avenue, close to the old Kennedy VA Hospital.

Sam Phillips, the owner of Sun Records, lived next door with his wife, Becky, and two sons, Knox and Jerry. Of course, Elvis Presley was a client of Sam's back then, in the early 1950s. I guess Elvis was about seventeen or eighteen when we first played football in my back yard.

Also, my father owned a used car lot across the street from Bellevue Park. For a time, while I was in grade school, my mother worked there part time a few days a month as the bookkeeper.

The car lot was located on the way south of town to Graceland. On several occasions, Elvis would stop at the lot and tell someone accompanying him to pick out any car on the lot to be theirs at Elvis' expense. During one of his stops just prior to Christmas 1961, he gave my father a pass to give to me so that I could attend the World Premiere of *Blue Hawaii* at The Malco in downtown Memphis. I had something better to do that evening, so I did not attend. I did see the movie on TV several years later.

Once my mother was no longer keeping books for my father, she worked for a Cadillac dealer in downtown Memphis. Elvis purchased his personal vehicles there. He always insisted that my mother share in the commission. Under no circumstances do I intend to convey that Elvis and I were good friends or buddies. According to my parents he was respectful and polite.

How did I get from playing football in my back yard with Elvis to coaching college football at Southwestern at Memphis?

After the holiday break in my senior year at Central High, during the 1958-1959 school year, I was summoned to the football office, where our head coach introduced me to Coach Mays, the head football coach of

Southwestern at Memphis. I was surprised to find my coach from junior high, Coach Fulghum, also present. They wanted to discuss my college plans. I told them that in all probability I would apply to Memphis State. Coach Fulghum reminded me that he was a commander in the U.S. Navy Reserves. He suggested that I consider joining the Naval Reserves with the objective of getting an appointment to the Naval Academy. But the deadline was past for the school year starting in the summer of 1959, so I would not be able to report to Annapolis until after the summer of 1960. Coach Mays, a former assistant coach at Central, said he would assist me in getting financial aid, so I could attend Southwestern for a year while awaiting my appointment. All went according to plan:

A. Coach Fulghum gained approval from my parents for the plan.

B. I joined the Naval Reserves in February 1959.

C. Coach Mays paved the way for me to get a leadership scholarship to Southwestern.

D. I applied and was accepted to USNA.

I knew next to nothing about the Navy other than what I might have remembered from the movies *Anchors Aweigh* with Frank Sinatra, and *Operation Petticoat*, starring Gary Grant and Tony Curtis. Eventually, though, the idea of attending the U.S. Naval Academy, seeing the world, and returning to Memphis after my service obligation was complete became my path forward of choice.

In the meantime, I would take courses at Southwestern aligned with those I would take in my plebe year at the Naval Academy, such as calculus, physics, and German. I also planned to play football and baseball. The NCAA rules in force at that time did not provide for loss of any eligibility due to participation in athletics at another college prior to enrollment at a service academy.

But what nobody counted on was that I fell in love with Southwestern in the first year and declined my appointment to the USNA. However, I was a member of the Navy, and under my contract I was obligated for twenty-four months active duty, and quite possibly my reporting date would not be delayed until I graduated. Again with the help of Coach Fulghum, I applied for and was accepted into the Reserve Officer Candidate Program and would spend eight weeks training in Newport, Rhode Island, after both my freshman and junior years of college. I changed my major to history, joined a fraternity, co-captained the football team my senior year, and co-captained the baseball team both my junior and senior years. The Southwestern baseball team captured the NCAA Division III National Championship my sophomore year. I was the catcher.

Upon graduation from Southwestern in 1963 it was time for my naval adventure to begin. But due to some administrative errors and associated Department of Defense budgetary problems, my commission and subsequent entry into active duty were delayed for an undetermined amount of time. One afternoon while visiting the Southwestern campus, I met the new head football coach. When he learned about my situation he asked if I would like to join his coaching staff until I received my orders to report for active duty. I'm not sure if I even asked him if it paid anything before I said yes. It did pay. I assisted the best I could, spending a good bit of my days reviewing film and scouting reports.

Then, on Monday, October 21st, I received a call to pack my seabag with all my Navy-issued enlisted uniform items and report to the administrative office at the Millington Naval Air Station, just north of Memphis, before the end of business that day. I was commissioned as an ensign that afternoon. I was ordered to report to the Little Creek, Virginia, Naval Amphibious Base for training. I was given a plane ticket for that Thursday and asked if I needed anything else. Since I had been required to turn in my seabag that contained now inappropriate uniforms for an officer, I asked about uniforms, but no one had an answer. The only comment was that it would be taken care of when I reached my duty station. I doubt if anyone meant an Admiral would personally take care of the problem, with his driver ferrying me to a Navy tailor in his car.

My active-duty obligation to the Navy was set to end in October 1966, which would be approximately three months after I returned to the United States from Vietnam. But the Navy assignment officer offered me the opportunity to extend my service obligation for three years and attend the Navy destroyer department head school in Newport, Rhode Island. My first and only ship assignment to date had been on a non-destroyer type ship. Since I had not previously served on a destroyer, I would be ordered for two months to a destroyer for indoctrination. I had to decide whether to go back to my hometown in Memphis, or attend destroyer school -- thereby putting off deciding what I would do after I grew-up for a little while longer.

In all probability what really tipped the scale was when my assignment officer asked for my choice of locations to perform my two-month indoctrination. It just so happened that Norfolk, Virginia, had destroyers, and it also had Bobbi. She was a girl I had met and dated when I was stationed in Norfolk, prior to my assignment to Vietnam. We had exchanged some letters while I was serving in Vietnam. So I picked Norfolk. My assignment officer said yes. That meant three more years in the military.

The ship I was assigned to in Norfolk was docked in port, instead of at sea, during most of my assignment. This allowed Bobbi and me ample time to spend together. Before I departed Norfolk for school in Newport in October of 1966, I asked Bobbi to marry me. She said yes, agreeing to join me on the journey through life. Our wedding was the best day of my life: January 21, 1967. We went on to have two fine sons, as well as two wonderful grandchildren.

Having remained in the Navy well beyond that "extra" three years, I assumed operational command in the summer of 1985 of the Navy's East Coast mine countermeasure forces. These forces consisted of ships, craft, helicopters, and explosive ordnance divers. In 1987, moored sea mines damaged several tankers operating in the Persian Gulf. The United States had to maintain free and unencumbered sea lanes through the Persian Gulf, to keep the flow of oil coming to the United States. So, aircraft were loaded. Ships were sailed. Equipment was sent, and people were flown. Dozens of mine sweeping vehicles and an eight-member staff were assembled and placed under my command. We were deployed to the Persian Gulf to execute Operation Earnest Will.

During my five months in command of this mine countermeasures task force, we swept the Persian Gulf in several Iranian-created minefields, with no injury to our personnel or equipment. It was a gut-wrenching experience to order mine hunting and sweeping ships and boats into mined waters. I paced and paced from the time the first manned unit entered a mine danger area, until all units had exited those waters safely. When employing the mine hunting and sweeping helicopters, it was a different matter. Being airborne, these units were not a "target" of the mines. Of course, through all of this I would often remember the four sailors who had lost their lives on PFC 4. As Christmas approached, another memory from that time in Vietnam came back around full circle. This time, it had a much more agreeable ending. As it turned out, Bob Hope was coming to visit our troops. And I was determined I would not miss his performance again, as I had done at the air base in Saigon on Christmas Eve of 1965. One of his shows was right onboard our ship, the USS *Guadalcanal*. And several days later, I even had the opportunity to actually meet and shake hands with Bob Hope at a party in Bahrain.

Upon my return from the Persian Gulf, I had to prepare a presentation for the Navy's senior officer, the Chief of Naval Operations, concerning Operation Earnest Will. I also briefed a panel of U.S. senators. It was arranged for me to give a pre-brief to a group of retired and active-duty military officers. During the question-and-answer portion, one of the retired officers asked if my command center contained any red phones. Yes, it was retired General Westmoreland asking the question. Then, at the conclusion of my briefing to the group of senators, the son of Admiral McCain

Jr., Senator John McCain III, asked if my uniform was a Frank Thomas & Sons product. The Senator then told the group that this was an inside joke. I never found out how he knew about the Frank Thomas uniform story, or his father's role. But it was certainly another full circle moment for me.

My association with Senator McCain did not stop there, though. My next duty assignment was in Washington, DC as a member of the Navy staff. My position was Director of the Expeditionary Warfare Division, which included the Navy's mine warfare forces. My consuming goal, based on my experiences in the Persian Gulf, was to get the sailor out of the minefield. Senator McCain helped all the way. Unmanned mine hunting and sweeping programs are still being refined, developed, and deployed to this day, all over the world.

From Elvis and Central High School in Memphis, to Vietnam, the Persian Gulf, and retirement in Virginia, it has been an enjoyable journey and an interesting education.

Jerry and Bobbi Manley and sons, 2022   Jerry Manley, 2022

6 - Virginia Leake Rowe

Mid-1960s - A Southern Woman in Washington, DC

The song that took 1960 by storm was "The Twist" by Chubby Checker. Everyone was dancing the night away to it. And then there was the follow-up song in 1961, "Let's Twist Again." I can still hear it: "Let's twist again, like we did last summer. Let's twist again, like we did last year." The dance it spawned of the same name was the craze of the early 1960s. Everywhere you looked people were doing "The Twist." Yet, I was one of the few who happened to luck into winning a Twist dance contest back then, while on a trip to Washington, DC with friends.

Of course, the dance contest was a lot of fun, and winning it was a thrill, but that time held more significance in my life than just my dancing triumph. That visit was when I fell in love with the "city on the Potomac." It was then and there that I decided I wanted to live in DC -- to move away from my Southern upbringing and my family in Memphis and strike out on my own in a city 876 miles away.

After I returned to Memphis from that DC trip and was back at my job at the Memphis Chamber of Commerce, my life there never felt the same. I loved Memphis. It was a great place to grow up and I had a lot of family there. However, in the years after that DC visit it was dawning on me that there was a whole new world out there, and I needed to spread my wings and give it a try. Washington was a beautiful and exciting city, with so much to see and do.

Now mind you, picking up and moving hundreds of miles away was not easy, but if I was going to see a little of the world outside of Memphis and meet new friends, this was the time to do it. I was not ready to get married in my twenties. Most of my friends had gotten married right out of high school or college. It was rare for someone at that time to leave their hometown to work elsewhere. People might have gone off to college, but they usually came back home to work or get married. It was also rare for someone at that time, especially a woman, to wait until they were thirty to get married. In fact, since all my brothers and sisters were married and had started their families before me, I knew they thought I was going to be the "old maid" of the family.

I did not know a soul in DC. I did not have a job or a place to live. I didn't have a clue. All I had was the friend of a friend who lived and worked in DC. Still, moving on and out was probably one of the best decisions of my life. And that friend of a friend turned out to be very instrumental in helping me find an apartment, a job, and my new life. So, in the mid-1960s, I packed up my car with my few belongings and took off for my new apartment in Arlington, Virginia. My new job, at the National Science Foundation, was across the Potomac River in DC. Living in the DC area gave me a chance to grow as a person, make lots of new friends from all over the country, and meet "the one."

The mid-1960s was the time of anti-Vietnam War protests in the streets, flag burnings, and civil rights marches. After living a very sheltered life in a mid-sized Southern city, this was all new to me. I was surprised that people would be so vocal, and act so hateful toward our military and our country. Growing up in the 1940s and 1950s, I thought life was so simple. I knew right from wrong. There was what I thought to be civility, accountability, and respect toward one another, our elders, our teachers, and those in authority. Our lives, as we knew it, were changing, and our generation had no idea back then how much and how fast it was going to happen.

I was homesick at first. I had only been away from home during the year when I went off to the University of Tennessee in Knoxville in 1959. My older brother was there, so it wasn't so bad. I jumped right into college life -- having a good time, dating, going to football games, pledging a sorority -- everything but studying. Then, it turned out that I had to withdraw from UT for financial reasons. So, I went back to Memphis to work, hopeful that I could finish college at Memphis State. That never happened, because once I started working and making my own money, I didn't want to go back to being a student. I have often wished there had been someone who pushed me more to finish college. Not getting that degree is one of my biggest regrets in my life. I would have loved to have gotten a law degree too and followed in my father's footsteps. However, two of my brothers did become lawyers and I am very proud of them.

I worked at the National Science Foundation for four years. I quit that job when two friends asked if I wanted to take the summer off and travel across country with them. Wow, what an opportunity to do something "wild and crazy." My mother was not too happy when I quit my job and hit the road. I sublet my apartment that summer, packed up my un-air-conditioned car, and took off to parts unknown with my two schoolteacher friends. We drove 10,000 miles that summer and were gone eight weeks. We drove from Washington, DC all the way down to Acapulco, Mexico, up the west coast of Mexico to Arizona, Las Vegas, over to California, and back across to DC. It was the trip of a lifetime. We're still talking about it more than fifty years later.

Once we returned to DC, my friends could go back to their teaching jobs, but what was I going to do? Fortunately for me, I got a job with my Congressman from Memphis, Dan Kuykendall, as his legislative assistant. Mr. Kuykendall was a conservative Republican who represented the ninth district in Memphis and served for four terms, until he lost to a Democrat in 1974 by only 744 votes. He was the first Republican to be elected to the ninth district in Memphis since 1872. He became known for being long-winded when he spoke on the House floor, which earned him the nickname, "The Tennessee Talking Horse." But Congress was a congenial place to work in those days. Regardless of whether you were a Democrat or a Republican, everyone seemed to get along.

It was an exciting time to work on Capitol Hill because of civil rights and Watergate. Kuykendall defended Richard Nixon at first, but later reconsidered his position on impeachment after Nixon refused to hand over evidence to the House. Shortly before Nixon's resignation, he supported impeachment. We had a great office, and we worked hard. It was the perfect job for me. I loved being in contact with our Memphis constituents, working on their behalf on "The Hill," a nickname for Congress.

It was during this time that I met my future husband, Ed. He had just arrived in DC to go to graduate school, and a friend of mine fixed us up on a blind date. He had graduated from West Point and had already served tours in Germany and Vietnam. He was coming to the DC area to get his graduate degree in political science from the University of Maryland. We dated for the next year-and-a-half before we decided to get married. I was thirty and he was thirty-two, and we were both ready to settle down and start a family. Neither of us had been married before.

Our wedding was during his spring break in 1972. After he graduated, we were supposed to head off to Command and General Staff School in Leavenworth, Kansas, but the Army threw us a curve ball. They decided they needed him in Vietnam once again and changed his orders. He was to report to duty on the first of July in 1972. The Army didn't care whether he had just gotten married or not, they shipped him off to war anyway. I'd always heard the saying, "If the Army wanted you to have a wife, they would have issued you one!" Fortunately, he came home to me after just seven months away. His tour was cut short after the U.S. began to withdraw troops in February 1973. The Paris Peace Accord was signed in April 1973, ending our participation in the war.

I guess you could say I was a war bride waiting for her husband to come home, and it was a tough seven months. The only way we could communicate was by writing, mailing audiotapes that we had recorded, or if we were really lucky, through a phone call which would cost an absolute fortune. The line was usually staticky and the call might drop, and we had to talk fast so we didn't spend a month's paycheck on just one call. Also, I was pregnant when he left. So, because of hormones I usually cried a lot when I heard his voice. His return wasn't quite soon enough for him to be there for our daughter's birth on the 29th of January 1973. He arrived a week after she was born. He found out he was a father from the Red Cross.

I was fortunate that he came home to me, but it was scary to think that he could have very easily been a casualty and I would have been left a widow after only a few months of marriage and with a new baby. Ed was a career Army officer. Combat assignments were to be expected when the country needed him. Those were tough times, because there was so much dissension about the war in those days. We had discussions about his time there and what he thought of the war. He had served his first tour in Vietnam as an advisor before we met. During that first tour in the mid-60s, he had seen a lot more action. His team was a small, tightly knit unit dependent on each other and their Vietnamese counterparts. He felt these tours enabled him to see the war from the viewpoint of the Vietnamese people. He has memories of working daily with the Vietnamese, dining with them and getting to know their families and beliefs. He also saw firsthand the horrors done to the Vietnamese villages and people by the Viet Cong, as well as the benefit of the civic works and medical assistance provided to them through U.S. aid. One thing I was curious to know was whether he had seen a lot of the drug use by our servicemen which was later depicted in movies such as *Good Morning Vietnam, Apocalypse Now*, and *Platoon*. He said he had not, because he was on small teams of four or five men who were busy with daily duties interfacing with the Vietnamese.

One good and positive thing that came out of the war, at least for us, was that, while in Vietnam on his second tour, my husband became good friends with his Vietnamese counterpart, a lieutenant commander in the Vietnamese Navy. In 1975, when South Vietnam fell to the North Vietnamese, Commander Le and his wife and four younger children, along with a cousin, fled Saigon on a fishing boat at a moment's notice, taking with them only what they could carry. The Le family included eight children, but they had to leave the four oldest ones behind in Hué with grandparents, because the older kids were at school, and they did not have a chance to pick them up before they left. It is hard to imagine dropping everything, leaving your mother country and four of your children, not knowing if you were ever going to see them again. If he had stayed, he knew he would have been killed for working with the U.S., and he feared for his family.

A U.S. Navy ship finally picked up the fishing boat and all those on board and took them to a refugee camp on Wake Island. In those days, if a refugee wanted to come into America, they had to have someone sponsor them and be responsible for getting them housed and resettled. Guess who got a collect call in the middle of the night asking if we would sponsor them? At first, my husband told the operator we didn't know anyone on Wake Island, but Commander Le was yelling "don't hang up, Ed, it's me, your Vietnamese friend." There was no way we could take on the full responsibility of sponsoring a family of seven. We didn't have the room in our home or enough money to help. We had moved back to DC for my husband's next tour in the Pentagon. So, the next day we went to our church, and they were more than willing to provide assistance to the family, both monetarily and physically. We put them up in the basement of the church and proceeded to settle them in by finding permanent housing, medical assistance, a job for the father, a car, clothing, and more. Their children ranged in age from nine months to seven years old.

The first job we got him was washing dishes at a country club. His next job was with a major grocery chain in the DC area. This was a god-send, because the job started out with our Vietnamese friend bagging groceries, then entering their management training program. After several years, he had worked his way up to manager of one of their major stores. Our friend worked hard, saved his money, and finally brought their other four children over from Vietnam ten years later, in 1985.

It still gives me chills to imagine living without your children for ten years. When the older children arrived, they couldn't speak English. The four youngest didn't know their older brothers and sisters, and they all had to relearn how to live together as a family, and in a foreign country. We were invited to the airport to greet the four oldest children when they arrived, and it is a moment I will never forget. To see this family who had been through so much both in Vietnam and here in the United States reunite their four older children with their four younger siblings was heart-warming. The youngest were too young to remember their older brothers and sisters. They were speaking English, going to American schools, and then these four strangers moved in with them. The parents had thought long and hard about how they were going to handle the situation, and before too long they were once again a family.

This is a real success story. One daughter graduated from William and Mary, another from the University of Virginia. One son graduated from the Naval Academy, two sons graduated from George Mason University, and one son got two master's degrees, one from Georgetown University and the second from the University of Rochester. We are so proud to know them and honored that we could be a part of helping their family make America their new home. We are still good friends with them today, and they never miss a moment to thank us for helping them get a new start in life.

Family is certainly important to me. I am blessed to be from a large family myself. I am one of six children, three boys and three girls. I am fifth in the pecking order. My father's family was from Collierville, Tennessee, now a suburb of Memphis. My mother grew up in Rosemark, Tennessee, a small town north of Memphis. My father was an attorney, and my mother went to secretarial school after graduating from high school. She wanted to attend a secretarial school in Memphis, and the only way she could do it was by living with her great-aunt in the city. Young women didn't go off on their own to live and work without some type of chaperone. Times had certainly changed by the time I left home. I just jumped in my car and took off for parts unknown. Who needed a chaperone? Not me.

My mother had met and married my father when she was nineteen. He was thirty-one -- eleven years older. They ran off and got married and didn't tell their parents until after the fact. My grandparents had a hard time accepting the marriage at first. Such an age difference was frowned upon back then, but from what I understand, my parents were madly in love with each other, so it didn't matter to either of them. The six of us were born during the next thirteen years.

My three brothers were all exceptional athletes, and I guess they came by it genetically, because my father played football at Washington and Lee University for two years in the 1920s. My great-grandfather played base-ball and organized the first baseball team in Collierville in the late 1800s. It was called the "Collierville Athletics." All three of my brothers went to college on full football scholarships -- one to the University of Oklahoma, and the other two to the University of Tennessee. My sisters and I did not get college degrees. It was the mindset back in the 1950s that it was more important for the boys to get a college education than the girls, and in my family, that was definitely the case.

Unfortunately, my father died in 1953 when I was eleven, leaving my mother a single parent with four children still at home. My mother did not have the financial resources to put her three daughters through college. I remember my mother telling me that I had to take typing and shorthand in high school, which would always provide me a means to get a job. I'm actually glad I did, because it came in handy when computers came into being. My mother was a strong, independent woman who kept the family together. She worked hard and established a career as what came to be called a headhunter in human relations -- getting other people jobs. She worked for a friend of hers, and then she bought the business from her friend several years later.

My high school class was on the cusp of a lot of changes that were beginning to happen at the end of the 1950s and the beginning of the 1960s. Since our class was born in 1941, we were not aware of World War II and what was going on around us. As we got older, we saw movies about World War II, with movie stars selling War Bonds, women working in factories to help the war effort, and the spirit of the nation coming together to support our troops overseas and the morale of our country. I remember my uncle coming home from the war when I was about five, and everyone making a big deal of it.

Memphis was the hot spot for Rock and Roll, the Blues, and Rockabilly as I became a teenager, although I don't think we appreciated it at the time. Carl Perkins, Jerry Lee Lewis, Johnny Cash, and of course Elvis Presley all lived and played music in Memphis during those years. I remember staying up late at night listening to the radio and calling our local DJ, Dewey Phillips, to request a song to be played or dedicated to that special someone. Most of us in high school didn't realize what we had in Elvis at the time, or at least I didn't. We kept hearing about this guy and his band who came from the "other side of town." We heard he was quite different from most of us, since he grew up in poverty.

Then, in the 1960s, the Vietnam War seemed to tear our country apart. The hippie generation came just after us. They believed in peace and free love. I think their generation did much to start the downward trend in actions of immorality among young people and lack of patriotism to our flag and country.

We grew up during a time when life seemed simple and fun. We didn't have to worry about much. We rode our bikes with only baseball hats on our heads, not helmets. We drank water from a garden hose, not a plastic bottle. We ate cupcakes, Twinkies, white bread, real butter, and bacon, and we drank drinks made with real sugar. We were always outside playing, not inside on a smart phone, iPad, or some type of computer. We experienced freedom, failure, success, and responsibility, and we learned how to deal with it all.

But despite the sometimes distressing changes since, I see my high school years as a fun and fulfilling time. We had wonderful teachers, great sport teams, sock hops (I guess that is where I perfected my dance skills), and lots of other activities. Friendships made during those three years have lasted more than sixty years. Even though I left Memphis in the mid-1960s, I have maintained special friendships with many of my high school class-mates, some going back to grade school. We take trips together, share experiences (good and bad), and relive all the fun times we had back then, and have had ever since. It seems we have come full circle from our high school days to attending our high school reunions, our last one being our sixtieth in 2019. One of our classmates has even established a class website with pictures, comments, and news. He has done a fantastic job in keeping the site up and running so we can stay connected.

A combination of the atmosphere of learning that Central High provided, the dedicated teachers, and the enduring friendships made it part of the foundation on which I built my life. It taught me discipline, self-confidence, respect for my elders, my friends, and our country, and instilled in me the desire to do something useful in life. Those really were some of the best years of my life. And the connections I still have to people from back then leave me feeling, even now in my eighties, that there will be more good times yet to come.

Virginia Leake Rowe, 2020   Virginia and Ed Rowe. 2022

7 - Jerry Conrad

1967 - The Vietnam War

Piloting an airplane over the Western Pacific Ocean at midnight, at 41,000 feet, with no lights around except the glow of the red instrument panel, you cannot believe the number of stars that are in the heavens. It is truly breathtaking. You come to realize just what a small speck each of us is in this big world. Man can build large machines, buildings, and other structures. But nothing can compare to the vastness of our universe. You look up into the black that goes on forever. My mind cannot comprehend infinity. But night flying over a vast expanse of ocean is close. It is not only inspiring, it makes you think. Who am I, and where am I going?

We were able to see this on many nights returning to Andersen Air Force Base in Guam in 1967 during the Vietnam War. That was at the start of the fifteen years I spent in the Air Force on active duty and in the Reserves, flying various types of planes.

As a young boy I had always liked airplanes. I built and flew models, wishing but not really believing I would someday be a real pilot, since it would be so expensive. Yet I got the opportunity to fulfill my boyhood dream. I think every young boy of my generation at some point wanted to be a pilot, policeman, doctor, or lawyer, or some exciting profession. If it had not been for Memphis State University and its Air Force ROTC program, I don't know where my career would have taken me. Because of that program, by the end of college in August 1963, I had gotten my private pilot's license. And after graduation, I got married and then headed to pilot training at Laughlin Air Force Base in Del Rio, Texas. Del Rio is a small border town in southwest Texas, which is in the middle of nowhere, west of San Antonio and right on the Mexico border. In October 1963, I began a grueling forty-five weeks of intense training there.

In pilot training, when I got to fly solo at night for the first time, I realized I had finally achieved the goal in the training syllabus. I had studied and flown to my best, and I was sure of myself. I had matured from a college student to a responsible adult. Flying teaches discipline, structure, and confidence. So, even though I was only twenty-three, I was ready to start my career and take on the world.

The last portion of our year, when we were close to graduation, the Air Force sent the training school a list of the aircraft for which they needed pilots. Then student pilots filled out a "dream sheet," listing which of those aircraft we wished to fly. The flight instructors and ground school instructors rated us as to which choice we were best suited to pursue. Our particular class was ready at a time when the Air Force needed more bomber and tanker drivers. That's why many of us ended up in the Strategic Air Command, and how I ended up flying bombers.

Upon graduation, I was given my wings. I was a pilot -- not a student pilot, but a real, honest-to-goodness pilot. Then, I found out my home base assignment was to be McCoy Air Force Base in Orlando, Florida. But before I could go there, I had to do some more training. First, I went to nuclear weapons school to learn all about nuclear bombs, then it was on to survival school, and finally to aircraft training school, to learn all about the

B-52. Nuclear weapons school was only two weeks long, survival school was a month long, and B-52 school was three months long.

When I finally arrived at McCoy as a Second Lieutenant in February 1964, I was the youngest pilot on the base, because my training had been shorter than usual. I was assigned to a B-52 with a crew of two pilots, two navigators, an electronic warfare officer who was also a navigator, and one enlisted man, the gunner. For the next few years, we flew training missions about three times a month and sat on call every other week for seven days in what they called the Alert Building. We were there to be ready to go to nuclear war, should the need arise. At that point, we were in the Cold War. Fortunately, that time never came. But the Vietnam era was just beginning then, and the Strategic Air Command was involved. That was when we started training to fly missions in support of the Southeast Asia conflict.

Our first six-month rotation began in October 1967. I flew an aircraft from McCoy to Andersen Air Force Base in Guam, an island in the Western Pacific that is thirty-seven miles long and seven miles wide at its widest point. I mostly flew a B-52, which usually meant lengthy missions. Our missions out of Guam lasted twelve hours each, and we flew once every third day for six months at a time, with one week off for rest and relaxation, which was in Hong Kong. That was exciting for me, since I was just a boy from Tennessee and had never entertained the thought of ever seeing that part of the world.

The name of our operation there was "Arc Light" and ran from 1965 to 1973. I was there toward the beginning. We flew bombing missions over enemy bases, supply routes, and troop routes in Vietnam. That environment could be full of danger, but also long stretches of quiet. I was flying in what others have called "boredom interspersed with moments of stark terror." Fortunately, the moments of terror were few and far between.

Each mission consisted of a preflight briefing, when we learned where we were going that day or night. Then there was takeoff, air refueling over the Philippines, flying into Vietnam, and then another six hours for returning. Most of the missions were pretty routine, but occasionally something different would happen. Early on, we flew mostly into South Vietnam, so we didn't have to worry much about being shot at. Except on one mission, intelligence was not aware that the North Vietnamese had installed some antiaircraft guns near where we were bombing around the Laos-Vietnam border close to the demilitarized zone -- an area between North and South Vietnam. This particular night, the weather was clear, and I could see Saigon way down south. All of a sudden, I saw three bright white flashes, like flashbulbs, but they were real explosives that went off right outside my window. Those antiaircraft guns could reach our altitude, and they began shooting at us. Fortunately, we were not hit, but it certainly got my attention. We returned and debriefed and told the intelligence people about the encounter. Thankfully, on the next mission in that area we went in at a higher altitude.

After we came back from that first six-month tour, I continued my upgrade training to become an aircraft commander. At this time I was only twenty-seven. I had been promoted to Captain and was happy doing my job as a copilot. I loved flying. Being able to move to the left, to the pilot's seat, was a big step in my career progression. One day, I got a call from the operations officer in the squadron, who asked if I thought I could handle my own crew. I emphatically said, "Yes." It appeared that another aircraft commander had had an accident, and they needed someone to take over that crew. We were getting ready to re-deploy to Southeast Asia for a second six-month tour, and since I had quite a bit of experience in the theater, they promoted me to that position, which I gladly accepted. It meant we were the youngest crew on Andersen Air Force Base.

These deployments would continue for the next two years. During that last year, I once again left for another six-month rotation back to Southeast Asia. This time I flew the twelve-hour missions out of Guam, and missions out of Kadena Air Force Base in Okinawa, which were about eight hours, and out of Utapo Royal Thai Air Force Base in Thailand that were only about three hours.

On one mission that was reasonably normal, we had just dropped our bombs and were returning to Kadena, when the navigator called and said we still had some stuck bombs in the bomb bay, We continued to landing, and when we got below 10,000 feet we depressurized, and he went back to check, and sure enough there was a bomb stuck in the bomb bay doors and a couple hanging in the bomb racks. After landing we were parked in a remote area and the bomb disposal personnel came and secured everything, and all was well.

About the only other tense moments were on a mission when we were cruising back to Guam at 41,000 feet. Everything was normal for about two hours, when we lost part of our electrical system. I was concerned that with four hours of flight left we might not be able to lower our gear. So, I informed the mission lead aircraft that we would be diverting to Mactan Air Force Base in the Philippines. After we got to a lower altitude, we slowed up and landed without incident. Even though we had rights to use this and other bases as emergency landing bases, I was a young aircraft commander and thought I might cause a huge political problem landing there. The base commander at Mactan met us and took me to call my wing commander to explain what had happened. To my relief, my wing commander was completely in agreement with my decision. We got to stay at Mactan for two days while they fixed our airplane before flying back to Guam. On our flight back to Andersen, my radar navigator discovered a new typhoon. This was before satellites were available for weather forecasting, so the weather people in the area were thankful to us for letting them know, and they sent a C-130 weather ship to check it out.

On January 1, 1970, I left Southeast Asia and didn't return. I had flown a total of 175 missions during my time there. To me that was a lot, but my squadron mates who had to stay flew many more.

The multiple long deployments played havoc with family life. When I had left on our second deployment, my daughter was only seven months old. Six months later, when I returned, she was already walking. So, I missed that milestone. But I did get back in time for her first birthday. Once my time in Southeast Asia was over, I decided that an Air Force career might not be in my best interests. I was still the youngest aircraft commander at McCoy Air Force Base -- a regular officer -- and had an almost guaranteed thirty-year career. I had everything going for me, but I lacked the security of being home with my family. So, I put in my resignation letter. I would continue to serve in the Reserves for a few more years, but my active duty career was over.

Before we deployed on my last rotation, I interviewed with Delta Airlines. By sheer luck and with God's help, the day after my service ended, I received a letter offering me a position. January 5, 1970 was the start of my thirty-one-year career with Delta, and I enjoyed every minute of it.

Starting over in a new uncertain career was a difficult decision. In the Air Force I had had security and advancement possibilities, but long separations and other difficulties. At the airline, I had control of when I wanted to move to another aircraft or change seats, based on my seniority. So, it was much more in my favor. Unfortunately, during the first few years at Delta, my first marriage ended. It was hard on me and my daughter. But I was blessed to have the opportunity to begin again.

While flying for Delta, I met a very beautiful lady, Annette, and we got married. We have two great sons together, Kris and Kevin, along with my daughter Kimberly. And now we have seven grandchildren and are extremely proud of them all. We have been married for more than forty years, and we couldn't be happier.

I retired from Delta in 2001 at the government mandated age of sixty as Captain of a 767-400. In my Air Force career and my Delta career I have flown all over the world and seen places I had only dreamed of seeing. But I couldn't give it up. After retiring, I started flying in the corporate world with a friend of mine who owned a Dassault Falcon, a small two-engine jet. I did this for another ten years and got to see a totally different kind of aviating. On a commercial airline, everything was preprogrammed. In the private world, you have to do everything yourself.

Someone once said, "find a job you enjoy, and you will never have to work." That's what happened to me. I have never worked a day in my life. I have only flown airplanes and have no regrets, and to this day if I get a chance to fly, I do it in a heartbeat. I believe that with God's help and a lot of luck I can unequivocally say that I have lived my dream. I ended my flying career with more than 28,000 hours of flying time. I have never had a crash. But I have lost some very fine colleagues, from either combat losses or other mishaps. I now pass the torch to the younger generation to continue to enjoy the rare opportunity to be in the group of those of us who get to call ourselves pilots -- because one of my sons decided to follow in my footsteps and is also pursuing a flying career.

Jerry Conrad, 1969

Jerry Conrad

8 - Melvin Kapell

1969 - The Moon Landing

It was Sunday, July 20, 1969, and the first manned spacecraft was set to land on the moon. My wife, Elaine, and I and our eight-month-old daughter sat together, glued to the TV in our small apartment in Houston, Texas, near the Manned Spacecraft Center. I was feeling nervous, and then excited, and then proud that I had played a small part in the mission at the time as a NASA engineer.

My responsibility at NASA Johnson Space Center was to certify the operation and performance of the communication systems -- the video, voice, and telemetry data -- between Earth and the spacecraft. We spent many years in the engineering division designing, analyzing, and testing the various components of those systems. We could have been called upon if there were communication issues during the mission. Fortunately, our systems worked as designed. I remember feeling gratified that our part was successful.

The actual landing on the moon was a little scary for those of us who knew what was really happening. Neil Armstrong spent time looking for a smooth landing spot with no boulders. When they finally touched down on the surface of the moon, they had only about ten seconds of fuel left. While in those final seconds of landing, Armstrong had a pulse rate of less than 90 -- but all of us who had worked on the Apollo program were close to blowing out our arteries. It was total silence at my home until Neil Armstrong spoke those words: "The Eagle has landed."

For me, those words signaling a successful touchdown of the Lunar Excursion Module on the moon were even more exciting than when he got out of the spacecraft with Buzz Aldrin behind him, actually set foot on the moon, and spoke the famous words: "That's one small step for man, one giant leap for mankind." The two astronauts spent nearly two hours walking the surface of the moon and collecting rock samples. We watched in awe, along with what seemed like the rest of the world. It was a wonderful time in the history of the nation, and I was fortunate to have been a part of it.

My interest in science began at a very young age. I had my first chemistry set in junior high school. I also purchased other chemicals to make gun powder, solid rocket fuel, and various concoctions. Fortunately, the old house still stands, and no one got hurt from my experiments. I was eleven years old when my neighbor's older brother, an engineer for an aerospace company, talked to his younger brother and me about sending a rocket to the moon. The idea at that time was unbelievable, it seemed like science fiction. But it spurred my interest in space exploration and engineering. An eighth-grade science teacher made science interesting by discussing what science can do to improve our lives. She brought her son, who worked for a TV station, to talk about split-screen TV pictures and advancements in television.

I was born in Memphis in 1941 and had a sister nine years older. She had married at twenty. So, at eleven, I became an only child and very spoiled. There was another child born before me who had passed away at nine months. It was never talked about. I only found out when my sister mentioned his passing. I was about twelve years old. My sister was young at the time and told me what she could remember. I think this is why I despise keeping secrets and always want to be open and informed.

My father was a salesman, and Mom was a housewife. We lived in a modest home on Willett Street in Midtown Memphis. I shared a room with my parents until my sister left home. The house was built in the early 1930s. The risers on the stairs to the attic were hinged. It was thought this was where liquor was hidden during Prohibition. After my parents passed away and we were cleaning out the house, we found a crockery jug hidden under the stairs. It sits on our fireplace today. Also on the fireplace mantle is a picture of my childhood home, painted by my sister. They remind me of my childhood days. There was an open field near the house where we played football and baseball. It is amazing we all survived without major injuries.

I went to kindergarten at Vollentine School when I was five. We were required to take naps every afternoon. But I was not a napper and was put in the corner as punishment for not sleeping. That was my first experience with stern teachers as authority figures. I started first grade at Snowden when I was six years old and stayed through ninth grade. I was not fond of school and loved recess and summer vacation. Those first years of schooling were hard, both emotionally and physically. Keeping up with the academics was a challenge for me, too.

There was bullying in my junior high years, along with gang fights, and I had my first introduction to racial and religious discrimination. Being Jewish, we often had to stay strong and resilient to cope. But at least once, some of my classmates thought being Jewish was an advantage. During Christmas at Snowden Junior High, participation was required in Christmas programs, unless you had different religious beliefs. So, some of my Christian classmates who thought being part of the programs was no fun tried to convince the teachers that they were Jewish to get out of them.

Still, what I am today is a result of the influences of my Jewish family. In 1903, my father's parents emigrated from a town in Russia called Dokshitz, near Minsk, to Memphis, where other family members had previously immigrated. The Jews who stayed in Russia were later killed by the Nazis. My father was born in Memphis in 1905. But my father's older brother was born in Russia. He was in Memphis by the time he started school. He told a story of a grade school teacher who asked where he was born. When he told her Dokshitz, she thought he said "dog shit" and sent him to the principal's office.

The small communities in Russia practiced Orthodox Judaism. My grandfather worked as a peddler after coming to America. He was a founding member of Congregation Anshei Sphard in Memphis. My father said the family would go hungry before he would work on the Sabbath. I remember going to my grandfather's house every Sunday. I was in the second grade and had not begun to study Hebrew, because Hebrew School did not start in Memphis until the third grade. My grandfather was very upset and angry because I had not yet started to learn Hebrew. Years later, though, my grandfather did not attend my Bar Mitzvah, because he would not ride in a car on the Sabbath and could not walk because of health. He died shortly after my Bar Mitzvah. I hardly remember my grandmother; she died when I was very young.

My father never finished high school because he had to work to help support the family. He was always bitter about not being able to finish school. He worked six days a week, twelve hours a day for about fifty-five years. He drilled into me the importance of finishing my education. My grandfather's and father's devotion to study and to never wavering from their beliefs, goals, and lifestyle influenced me to work hard to achieve my goals and never give up.

My mother was born in Nashville. Her parents had emigrated from Hungary in the early 1900s and passed away before I was born. My mother's father, whom I was named after, was said by many family members to be a compassionate and kind person. I don't know if I can ever achieve that status, but perhaps it influenced me to be compassionate and caring. Every summer we would go to Nashville to visit my mother's extended family. We stayed with my aunt and uncle. My grandmother had died when my mother was thirteen. So, my mother lived with her sister and brother-in-law until she got married. She never had the opportunity to finish high school. Both parents and grandparents educated themselves by reading and studying. We would visit my mother's brother who owned a grocery store in midtown Nashville. I loved to ride in his truck, because no one I knew owned a truck in Memphis. A few years ago, my wife and I visited Nashville. I searched for my aunt and uncle's home, which was difficult, since all the street names had changed. I was able to find the street, and the property had become an RCA studio on Nashville's Music Row. During this trip we searched for the location of my uncle's grocery store, which is now a shopping center located across the street from a major hospital. We also went to the Jewish Cemetery to pay our respects to the family and research family history.

During my high school years, B'nai B'rith AZA, a Jewish youth organization, was a big part of my social and religious life. I enjoyed the sports and social activities and made many friends for life. There was a large group of Jewish students at Central High who congregated for lunch. I remember during Passover there were kosher Cokes in the Coke machine. My Jewish friends were hard-working, ambitious students; most became professionals in many disciplines.

Starting the tenth grade at Central High School was time to get serious about education. Our careers depended on the classes we picked. I enrolled in math and science classes. I disliked classes such as English, Language, and History, which were not easy for me. Students with those college majors did not have careers or jobs developing rockets and capsules to go into space. Only a few of my classmates majored in science or engineering in college.

My family did not have funds for me to go out of town to college. Since I wanted to study engineering, I applied to Christian Brothers University. It was the only school in the area that had an engineering curriculum, and it had an excellent electrical engineering program, with a reputation for its graduates doing well. I discovered later, after working, that I had better math skills from this small college than many students from larger universities. The school was very respectful of other religions, but that was not true of some students.

During one summer, I had a summer intern job at Martin Aircraft Company in Denver, Colorado, in the foothills of the Rocky Mountains. I got to tour many beautiful sites in the Rocky Mountains. I would have liked to work there, but the winters were too cold and harsh. Also, Martin was contracted by the Defense Department to build the Titan Intercontinental Ballistic Missile. Only a while after that summer did I realize I had been working on a missile capable of destroying a city and killing thousands. That was a sobering realization, and it helped me decide I didn't want to work in that field of engineering. I wanted to be part of expanding our understanding and exploration of space.

I graduated with a Bachelor of Science in Electrical Engineering in 1963 and began looking for a job. The United States was not yet drafting young men for the Vietnam War, so I was not concerned about being drafted. I applied for a job at NASA Johnson Spacecraft Center in Houston and was offered a job in design and testing of space communication systems for the Apollo mission. Once the U.S. began drafting men, I had an exemption because of my job, which was considered essential. During the hiring process, a security background check was done, including interviews with friends and neighbors. I'm sure they wondered what kind of trouble I had gotten into for them to be interviewed about me like that. Concurrent with my job at NASA, I enrolled in a Master of Science in electrical engineering program at the University of Houston and graduated in 1967.

Moving to Houston was like going to a foreign country. Three languages were spoken, English, Spanish, and "Spanglish." A big city with massive freeways and big open spaces was a big change from living in Memphis.

But the brightest moment was in January of 1966, when Elaine and I met in Houston. We were set up as a blind date by her great-aunt, who had lived in Memphis for many years. So, she was also a friend of my family. On our first date we went to a house party. After that date we spoke every night. We had several more dates, and by March I knew she was the one. I proposed after we attended the play *Barefoot in the Park* at a local theater. We were engaged in March. In April, during Passover, we drove to Memphis to meet my parents. We were married in August 1966 at Congregation Beth Yeshurun in Houston.

In the beginning at NASA, I worked on testing and design of the Apollo program space communication systems. This encompassed two-way audio, video, and data for the status of the space vehicle and health of the astronauts. The technology systems for the Apollo communication systems were typical 1960s analog designs, unlike broadband digital systems today.

After Apollo, the next major NASA mission was the Space Shuttle, whose design began in about 1969, around the time of the moon landing. My engineering directorate was responsible for the design, development, and test of the digital communication systems. This consisted of high-speed data, voice, and video, and using orbiting satellites for relaying communications. It was an early version of the digital communication used today in television, internet, computers, and cell phones. It required many years and government funding for research and development.

We were always anxious and tense about watching the shuttle lift-offs and landings. The shuttle made many successful missions providing transportation for Earth-to-orbit crew and cargo. The *Challenger* and *Columbia* Space Shuttles were lost because of technical failures. I was in a design meeting for the International Space Station when the *Challenger* exploded in 1986. The meeting was halted, and everyone was in shock and disbelief. With the *Columbia* disaster in 2003, communication was lost with the shuttle. Those were harrowing times for all of us at NASA.

I was a member of NASA's initial design team for the International Space Station. The basic design of today's orbiting space station is based on the work of our team. While working on the space station's communication systems design, we cooperated with our international partners, including the Japanese, Europeans, Russians, and Canadians. Engineers tend to use many acronyms and slang words, which caused confusion with our international partners.

The shuttle and space station depended on relay satellites for broadband digital communication to and from earth. Similar satellites are still used today to relay video and data throughout the world. Yet things have advanced so quickly that these days there is more computer technology in your cell phone than we had going to the moon.

Working at NASA was not always smooth sailing. One reason Apollo was so successful was that Congress gave NASA continuous funding, and there was no interference across several presidential administrations. In later space programs, some in Congress decided they were better engineers than we were, and they tried to change the focus of the program. This caused numerous delays and cost overruns. There were delays caused by technical and operational failures. Aerospace programs are risky and difficult and technically challenging. One thing I learned was the word *expert* is used too liberally. Too many people, such as politicians, who claimed to be experts in their field also believed they were qualified as experts in other disciplines.

I have been asked many times why we went to the moon and why we continue space exploration. I usually answer by pointing out that, historically, when past societies became stagnant and stopped being innovative, they collapsed. Progress is essential to improve our lives and society. Each year, NASA published a book of spinoffs from space technology. Each book described advancements in fields such as medicine, the environment, food technology, computer systems, communications, safety, security, and more.

After the launch of the Russian satellite *Sputnik*, President John F. Kennedy realized the engineering and scientific talent in the United States was lagging behind other countries. Deciding to go to the moon helped create more interest in science and technical jobs. Engineering professionals were in demand. This lasted until President Richard Nixon brought the Apollo program to an end. Funding for the space program became more political. NASA was able to continue at a much slower pace by developing the Space Shuttle and Space Station. College enrollment in science and engineering dropped. Students turned to business degrees and law school because of higher wages and more stable jobs.

However, even among professional people, there was racism, anti-Semitism, and discrimination against women in the technical fields. They were not encouraged or counseled for career opportunities. For example, throughout my childhood and young adult years, women were considered less capable students with few opportunities. In the late 1990s, Congress was pushing NASA to hire more minority scientists and engineers. There were few minority or women applicants, and NASA had to compete with the private aerospace industry, which offered better pay. Today, interest in science and engineering is enhanced since STEM is being promoted in high schools and universities.

One day, a young engineer came into my office to chat. He said he was engaged to be married to a Jewish woman. Not being Jewish, he was concerned about meeting her parents. When he went to meet them, it was obvious they were disappointed. However, when he told them about his father, who was a famous surgeon on the East coast, and about his two brothers who were physicians, it seemed to set them at ease. Jewish families often encouraged their children to be doctors or to marry one. So, they must have thought, at least she is marrying into a doctor's family. Luckily, my parents and my wife's parents were okay with me pursuing an engineering career.

Elaine and I have been together for more than fifty-five years. We've been fortunate to have a healthy and prosperous life. We have two children, one who is analytical and the other who is artistic. Our daughter is a graduate of the University of Texas with a BA in mathematics. She is married and has two daughters. She and her husband live in Austin. She works analyzing and testing computer software for insurance and financial companies. Our son is married and lives in Virginia. He is a graduate of the University of North Texas with a BA in music. He received a Masters of Sacred Music from the Jewish Theological Seminary and is a cantor for a Conservative synagogue in Maryland. I don't even sing well in the shower. His talent is inherited from Elaine's grandmother. She was classically trained in opera, in Berlin. She was not allowed to perform because it was not appropriate for women to be on stage in those times.

After my mother passed away in 1984, my father spent several years in the Memphis Jewish Home, a senior care facility. After he moved out of my childhood home, we finally sold it, and we closed the sale in June 1986, exactly fifty years to the day from when my parents had purchased it. Then, in 1987 my father died.

Through the years, I had worked on the Apollo, Space Shuttle, and Space Station programs. Later, my responsibilities were more focused on contract management, working with aerospace companies. Then in June 2005, after forty-two years at NASA, I retired. Elaine had retired a few years earlier after working in banking and lending.

As a teenager I read Richard Halliburton's *Complete Book of Marvels* that described great wonders of the world, such as the Taj Mahal, Mount Everest, the Great Wall of China, Machu Picchu, Angkor Wat, the Monastery in Tibet, and many more. They were outstanding engineering structures of those times, made with the primitive tools that were available. It was a dream of mine to visit those places.

Since our retirement, Elaine and I have been fortunate to travel extensively and have gotten to visit many of the wonders of the world I read and dreamed about as a kid from the *Book of Marvels*. We have also met many people of different cultures and nationalities. I even met one of my father's cousins who lived in Cape Town, South Africa. He had many family pictures and discussed family history. That part of the family emigrated from Russia to South Africa while others came to the United States in the early 1900s. We also try to visit Jewish sites wherever we go. We often traveled with my NASA co-worker and his wife. And of course, an always exciting travel experience was to go to Cape Kennedy in Florida to watch the launches of Apollo and Shuttle missions.

Once, while in South Africa on a game viewing drive in a national park, we stopped in an open area where you could see clearly for miles. It was beautiful, only natural light and crystal-clear skies. We observed an object moving rapidly across the sky. Everyone wondered what it was. I knew, telling everyone that it was the International Space Station. What an exciting way to close out a career, seeing the success of my efforts in space, from the Earth.

On July 27, 2019, a NASA Johnson Space Center award was presented to the original small group of engineers, including me, who had established the electronic systems test laboratory at Johnson Space Center in 1964. The facility was designed to test space communications systems simulating transmission conditions between Earth and space. It was the only facility in the United States that could do this type of testing and evaluation of communication systems. It was built to test the Apollo system, and it has also been used to test the Space Shuttle, Relay Communication Satellite, and Space Station systems. It is able to verify designs and correct problems prior to launches, preventing failures. It is still being operated today. I am very proud of that achievement.

A bedroom in our home has many pictures and mementos of my career at NASA. It was a great job at a wonderful time in the history of this nation. I am honored that I contributed to the advancement of technology in the United States and the world. I never imagined that I would be part of a program of such significance.

Also, in the hallways in our home, we have pictures of family members dating back to the late 1800s. Each one has its own story. All had the desire and courage to seek a better life for themselves and our family. We must continue to encourage our families to always seek a better, rewarding, and happy lifestyle. To me, at eighty, this is life's two-minute warning, signaling we should take advantage of the time we have left -- no overtime allowed. I am grateful that, so far, Elaine and I and the rest of our family have been blessed with happiness and health, and with so many wonderful opportunities.

Melvin Kapell,
Shenandoah Valley National Park, 2015

Melvin and Elaine Kapell
and family, 2021

9 - Freyda Tresan Roth

1971 - Moving to Israel

It was June 1967, and I was living in New Orleans with my husband and our two children. But my immediate concern was the impending Six-Day War between Israel and invading forces from surrounding Arab countries. It was a frightening prospect because there were threats of annihilation of Israel. Since the establishment of the country in 1948, there had never been such a dire situation with the risk of extinction. The emotional impact of such possible consequences had a tremendous effect on me personally.

At that time, I was completing my two-year term as president of the New Orleans Chapter of Hadassah, the Women's Zionist Organization of America, whose main goal was to raise funds for the Hadassah Medical Organization in Israel. During the course of my presidency, I had met a number of people from Israel and become very familiar with the country, its life, and its needs. And shortly after the war, one of the visiting speakers asked me, "Have you ever considered moving to Israel?" Well, I had never even thought about it, and no one I knew had even broached the subject. I felt that I was helping this developing country by volunteering my time and donating money to maintain hospitals and programs providing a haven for homeless immigrants and exiles. When I mentioned to my husband, Malcolm, the novel idea of our moving to Israel, he said he thought it was a wonderful idea and the only place he would ever consider living besides New Orleans. Let's do it! I had been the active Zionist, but he was the idealist who enabled our move.

This had become a period of tremendous immigration to Israel from the free world, and we too felt the need to help ensure Israel's survival. This was the essence of Zionism, defined in Wikipedia as "both an ideology and nationalistic movement among the Jewish people that espouses the re-establishment of and support for a Jewish state in ... Israel."

With this belief in our minds and hearts, in June 1971 we left the peaceful and secure country of our birth and moved, with our three children, to a distant land engulfed in strife and war -- hoping for a peaceful future for all involved. We lived for five months in an absorption center, where we studied Hebrew six days a week. It was not always an easy adjustment -- a real culture shock. But the Israeli people were warm and helpful to us in every way, and we slowly began to fit in and feel at home. Our friends and family in the States were sure we would return within a year, but we had made a commitment, and we never considered the option of returning to the United States. My parents were proud, while my in-laws blamed my Zionist activism over the years. They were not happy we were leaving New Orleans for such an "unsafe place" and taking their grandchildren as well. But they realized over time the strength of our commitment.

After living for six months in an absorption center and another five months in the small town of Parde Hanna, we moved to Haifa, where my husband invested in a commercial laundry business with another new U.S. immigrant, who had been in a similar business in Pittsburgh. This was in 1973, shortly before the Yom Kippur War, and the business went bankrupt due to the resulting commercial slowdown of the economy.

Our exposure to war was another first-time experience for us. Having come from a peaceful and safe existence in the United States and the six-year calm after the euphoric success of the Six-Day War, we were not psychologically prepared for the Yom Kippur War in 1973. Israel was attacked simultaneously from Syria in the north, Jordan in the east, and Egypt in the south. Without warning, there were sirens all over the country at 2 p.m. on our holiest day of the year. Not really understanding what was happening, we and our dog joined the neighbors from our building of six apartments in the built-in bomb shelter in the basement and waited for the all-clear. Several sirens called us to the shelter over the next week. However, after the initial fright, we eventually adjusted to the situation, though always with fear and trepidation.

My husband wanted to join the troops in the Golan Heights but was not allowed since we were not yet full Israeli citizens. New immigrants had to wait three years to automatically become citizens without losing their American citizenship. Somehow he managed to volunteer his services as a civilian driver of needed goods and ended up being strafed but unharmed by Syrian MIGs on the way to the fighting zone.

Unfortunately, over the years, we had other experiences which exemplify the war-peace existence of life in Israel. The most unforgettable for me was the Gulf War in 1991, when there was a threat of chemical warfare in which everyone had to carry personal warfare kits to work and school, with full-face gas masks and anti-gas atropine syringes. In case of attacks, when we heard sirens, we were to don the masks and run to sealed rooms. So surreal! I remember sitting in our sealed bedroom, with tape and plastic on the windows and wet towels around the doors, and listening to the radio to hear where the bombs were hitting. There was no advance warning at that time.

Suddenly, on one occasion, there was such a roar that I was sure a Scud missile was coming through the window, but it turned out to be the unbelievably loud boom of a Patriot missile shooting down the Scud.

While this was all happening, we were on the phone with my family in the States, who were relaying information from CNN before we heard it from our own radio stations, which were avoiding saying exactly where the bombs were falling for security reasons. In our panic, my husband injected our German Shepherd with the anti-poison gas atropine since she did not have a mask. She just fell asleep on the bed next to us and woke up a while later. To find myself and my family in such an unbelievable situation was truly an eye-opener.

From the very beginning of our move to Israel, I was aware that such an event was possible, but I lived in both a state of denial of just how volatile our environment was, and a state of fulfillment at being in Israel in the first place. I see now that this was actually a continuation of the disconnection and insularity of our previous lives in the United States. I began to realize how protected and unaware my generation had been from the realities of life as I was growing up. I thought of the issues which had been so marginal to my life before moving to Israel, such as World War II, the Holocaust, anti-Semitism, racism, poverty, and human rights.

I was a nice little Jewish girl, born in 1941 and raised in Memphis. In terms of my family background and our financial situation, I could not be defined as a JAP -- a Jewish American Princess, a derogatory term used in the last half of the twentieth century to describe young, indulged, Jewish women and girls from families that had lots of money. But in every other respect, I feel like I had a charmed life. In spite of World War II, which was raging when I was born, I felt secure and loved with a large extended family and many friends. I had a happy childhood in a friendly, middle-class neighborhood.

My family roots on both sides were Eastern European. In search of an easier life and freedom from persecution in the early 1900s, my mother's parents came from Radom, Poland -- first to Montreal, Canada. They arrived with one son who was joined later by five sisters, the second of whom was my mother, born in 1911. Subsequently, they moved to Pine

Bluff, Arkansas, when her father, my grandfather, decided to open his own grocery store there with a fellow "landsman" -- a friend from his former home in Poland. However, they eventually relocated to Memphis, to have easy access to kosher meat according to Jewish dietary laws. Each child had a specific function in the family, either working in their grocery store on Mississippi Avenue, where they lived upstairs, helping with the cooking and baking and upkeep of the home, or working outside the family business or studying. My mother learned fine arts at Tech High School and proved to be a very accomplished artist and calligrapher. She even won first place in a contest sponsored by the Memphis *Commercial Appeal* newspaper for advertisement illustrations.

My father was born in 1908 in Chita, Siberia, where his father was serving in the Russian Army as a tailor, having been conscripted from his home in Belarus. His family immigrated to the United States when he was age three by way of New York City, at which time the family name was changed from Treshansky to Tresan. (As I was growing up, I was always so embarrassed whenever any mention was made of the word "treason," since its pronunciation was too close for comfort to Tresan for me.) The family lived for a while in New York, where his two sisters were born. Then, on the recommendation of other landsmen who had found work and good living conditions in Memphis, they moved, along with my father's grandmother Freida, for whom I was named. For many years my grandparents ran a kosher delicatessen at the corner of Main Street and Jackson Avenue.

By going to night school, my father became an accountant. He held many different day and night jobs managing small private company accounts. Eventually, he began working for Julius Lewis Clothiers, becoming their comptroller and officer manager, and remaining until his retirement in 1974. We were closely affiliated with the Lewis family over the years, and I have very fond memories of being invited to their home every Christmas Day. This was a tradition of theirs even though they were Jewish, but which we did not celebrate. I was fascinated by their lovely home, the eggnog, the Christmas fruitcake, and the beautiful gifts they gave to me, my brother, and my sister.

As a child, I remember visiting my father at work in this high-class department store and thinking that it all belonged to him. What did I know? Another misconception that resulted from his affiliation with such a prestigious concern was that we could afford the high-priced quality clothing we purchased there, never knowing of the 40 percent discount he received as a senior employee. I felt sorry for friends who had to buy at lower-priced shops. I now see that I was being an unaware snob.

For me, money was never a conscious worry; I never felt deprived. However, my father's stringent frugality is instilled within me to this day. For example, prescription sunglasses were a nonessential "luxury" item that I had to buy for myself. We were able to take a two-week family vacation every year by car. But my siblings and I were not able to attend sleep-away summer camps, as they were deemed too expensive. My little sister got my outgrown clothes, and I was the lucky one who got the new items.

My father's only extravagances were the fine Hart Schaffner Marx suits he wore in keeping with his prestigious position, and a new car -- usually a Buick -- every couple of years. In keeping with his financial conservatism, he and my mother bought a U.S. Savings Bond every month of their lives no matter their situation. My mother did not work at all until I left for college, leaving only my sister at home. In my high school years, I worked as a relief cashier in some of the departments at Julius Lewis on occasional Saturdays. Except for one stint as an assistant summer camp counselor, this was my only paid working experience before moving to Israel at age thirty.

Being Jewish was a significant factor in my Memphis life, and this is the reason my experiences differed from the majority of my neighbors and classmates. In the Jewish community in Memphis -- around 10,000 people at that time -- there were three Orthodox congregations, one Conservative congregation, and one Reform congregation. Those who affiliated with the Orthodox and Conservative synagogues were likely to be more observant of the Jewish holidays and traditions in contrast to those of the Reform temple. So, some Jewish students would be absent during Jewish holidays while others would not. Some observed kosher dietary laws -- in varying degrees -- or did not take part in school social events or activities on Saturdays, the Jewish Sabbath.

I felt secure being Jewish and was comfortable belonging to a small Orthodox congregation and observing holidays and a kosher home. We were what you would call "traditional" but not religious according to strict Jewish laws. That means we would eat out occasionally at non-kosher restaurants and would ride and use electricity on the Sabbath. My father had no choice since he always had to work on Saturdays. However, we always had the traditional Friday night Sabbath dinner, lighting candles and saying the blessings over the wine and food. We also observed all the Jewish holidays during the year. Even though Christmas is not a Jewish holiday, I loved singing the carols at school, enjoying all the decorations and holiday cheer, and helping my neighborhood girlfriend decorate her family tree. I never felt torn or sacrilegious by appreciating non-Jewish customs.

In my early school years, I attended Sunday morning school to learn Bible stories about the Old Testament and also went to afternoon Hebrew classes, where I learned to read but never speak or understand the language. I also celebrated the traditional Bat Mitzvah ceremony for Jewish girls at age twelve.

During my junior high years, I started attending weekly, Zionist-oriented, Young Judaea meetings, learning Israeli folk dancing and songs and traditions. I also attended occasional weekend gatherings, with our movement leaders being Jewish high school students. So I was solidifying my identity as I became immersed in my Judaism and Zionism while also acknowledging the fact that I was a minority in a Christian-dominated society.

In junior high, I also became a member of a Jewish sorority and was also chosen twice to be Sweetheart of a Jewish fraternity. I was not a vivacious, sociable person, but it appears that I was known as an intelligent, respected, attractive-enough person with a good reputation. Even though I never saw myself as someone different, it was as if I was put on a pedestal among my Jewish peers. But I just wanted to be considered one of the gang.

A majority of the Jewish students did not date non-Jewish students. This was very often due to parental dictates and did not necessarily reflect the feelings or religious commitments of the students themselves. In fact, in high school I had a close relationship with a male, non-Jewish class-mate. We probably would have dated if I had been allowed. But I was not even allowed to invite him to my home to study together. Once, when my parents were out for the evening, he came over anyway, and he had to rush out the back door when they arrived home early. I was not punished when they found out about my "indiscretion." They said they trusted me not to do this again. And I didn't.

During this time, I made good grades in a full academic curriculum and won honors. My brother was older than I by four years and had attended Central and won many awards, in addition to being chosen Most Intelligent in his senior year before going to Yale. So, I had very big shoes to fill in his wake. I believed I was not as smart as he was, but I did succeed in my studies, was co-editor of our yearbook, was a member of the Honor Society and the Quill and Scroll, and also served as an ROTC sponsor. My extracurricular activities at that time were mainly in the Jewish youth organization world, involving leadership positions, travel, and diverse responsibilities. Right after graduation, I finally got to go to summer camp, where I had the best experience of my life as a co-counselor at the B'nai B'rith summer camp in Pennsylvania. I knew then for sure that I loved to work with other people. By nature, I am a people pleaser, and this opportunity to give of myself and receive pleasure and appreciation in return set the pattern for my life ahead.

In reflecting now on my state of mind and that of my classmates during our years at Central, I realize that we had lived through an era of innocence and insulation -- a lack of awareness. We were interested primarily in continuing in the cocoon of our own personal and unchallenged spheres, and not with the developing concerns of society and the world at large which would identify the coming decade with issues such as racism, Vietnam, human rights, drugs, social protests, and feminism.

I graduated from Central and was accepted to Vassar, Wellesley, and Newcomb College, the women's college at Tulane. I didn't receive offers of financial aid, except from Newcomb in New Orleans. So, that's where I went. This was also when I chose to assert my presence and be called "Freddie," the name I was always called by my family. "Freyda," the name given to me at birth, was always mispronounced and misspelled, and I never really liked it anyway.

At Newcomb I made the Dean's List the first semester and was also president of my sorority pledge class. I liked my college friends and the excitement of New Orleans, but I did not find the academic life there very challenging or fulfilling. At the beginning of my second semester, I met my husband to be, and soon after that my life changed completely. We married in July 1960, and I bowed to my mother's mantra that my primary role as a woman and a wife was to be available for my husband. That was the end of my formal studies, soon to be replaced by motherhood, community service, fundraising, volunteering, and involvement in Jewish organizations.

I still wonder what I could have achieved if I had continued to study and had delayed becoming a wife at age eighteen, and a mother at twenty. My way of thinking and the path I took were partially a result of my comfort and security to stay within the confines of the familiar -- and the lack of a female professional role model to strive for something else. Later, as I established my independence from the very personal insular attitudes of my family and generation and found a new life and perspective, I realized that I had no desire to return to the narrow, community worldview of my life in Memphis. And that ultimately influenced our decision to move to Israel and then not to return to the States as well.

When we came to Israel in 1971, the overall population was about three million people. Today there are more than nine million citizens, of whom approximately 74 percent are Jewish, 21 percent Muslim and Christian Arabs, and 5 percent from other ethnic groups such as Druze, Bahá'i, Circassian, and Samaritans.

We had to confront and accept many issues over the years. As I mentioned, our religious involvement in the United States had been traditional and partially observant. But surprisingly in Israel at that time, it was a black-or-white situation for Jews, you were either fully religious or not religious at all. There was no in-between. There are separate religious and secular school systems and no public transportation or commerce on the Sabbath. The Jewish holidays and the Sabbath on Saturday are designated as sort of national holidays for everyone -- including the Arab Muslim and Christian populations. Most nonreligious or secular Jews do not attend religious services at any of the many neighborhood synagogues or follow the religious traditions, choosing to observe these holidays as they please. Since Saturday is the only day off after a six-day work week, our family chose to maintain our lifestyle as nonreligious Israelis so we could enjoy this family day when we went touring, to the beach, boating on the Sea of Galilee, or spending time with friends. In such a strict situation, we found that we could not identify as religious Jews and send our children to a school where relaxed religious observances were not understood or accepted.

Even though Jewish tradition had been comfortable and close to us in the past, we slowly moved away from that aspect of our lives. Today, I still light candles and have a traditional Friday night Sabbath dinner when my family is present, but we stopped having a kosher home or attending synagogue long ago. Even though each of my children had the traditional Bar or Bat Mitzvah ceremony at ages twelve or thirteen, it is my regret that they and their children are missing the warm connection and traditions of Jewish life that I had in my past, and that we no longer experience as nonreligious Israelis.

Another fraught issue now in Israel is the fact that the religious and ultrareligious parties control government policies concerning marriage, burials, military service, Sabbath public transportation and commerce, access to the Western Wall in Jerusalem, land sovereignty, and recognition of Diaspora Jewry. These facts cause much resentment toward those who want to impose their beliefs on everyone. An unfortunate and explosive conundrum for our country. And for me it is also a sad state of affairs that there is a lack of compromise on these issues.

By 1973, I had begun working at the newly established IBM Israel Research and Development Center, the first of its kind outside the United States. I was hired because of my good English skills. We started with twelve staff members -- all PhDs in computer or related sciences -- and I left thirty-one years later with 1,200 employees on board. My responsibility at the beginning was editing the research technical reports that were sent abroad to our working partners. This evolved into other administrative responsibilities while I took relevant courses at the Technion, Israel Institute of Technology. I loved my work over all those years and felt gratified in my accomplishments.

While still working at IBM in 1997, I started volunteering once a week at Amcha, a nonprofit organization providing social and psychological support for Holocaust survivors and the second generation. During my life in Memphis, the Holocaust was a distant issue that did not affect me personally, as far as I knew. While reading *Exodus* by Leon Uris during the summer after my graduation from Central, I was introduced for the first time through historical fiction to the unbelievable horrors of the Holocaust, and this affected me profoundly. After that and until today, I have read hundreds of books on the subject. Even though I had met some survivors who came to live in New Orleans when I was living there, I did not have the awareness or opportunity to get to know them and to inquire about their origins and experiences. Only after moving to Israel did I become exposed to this very integral segment of society here. I also learned that distant cousins I never knew -- a family of five from Poland -- were among the six million who were killed.

By the end of 1951, 687,000 Holocaust survivors, from both European and Arab countries, had been absorbed into the state of Israel. Today, approximately 190,000 are still alive. I am fortunate to know and to have known a small number of these survivors and have found their resilience and life force to be an uplifting experience.

My role as the "teacher" at Amcha is to prepare the weekly, hour-and-a-half sessions using material from books, current events, and the internet, and also to give Holocaust survivors easy and entertaining activities and homework. It is a casual session with opportunities for them to express themselves with a lot of laughter and interaction. It was my recent project to write a book as a testimonial to these people I have been honored to know. I distinctly remember each name and individual and wanted to share the stories of more than fifty of the survivors, the majority of whom are no longer alive. It was my goal to give personal tribute to the strength and fortitude and humanity of each and every one who survived and built a new life. Knowing them has truly enriched my life. It has been my privilege.

My three children, their respective spouses, and now eight of my nine grandchildren have served in the Israel Defense Forces. The youngest is seventeen and will serve his three-year duty as well. I feel that this is an honor as well as an obligation for each of them

Despite knowing the need for Army service in Israel, I clearly remember my elation on hearing of the upcoming visit of Anwar Sadat to Israel in 1977. I ecstatically thought, "Oh, maybe now there will be peace, and there will be no need for our children to go into the Army." I feel equally optimistic today now that several other Arab countries have decided to normalize relations with Israel. I am hopeful this will eventually bring peace to all of the Middle East. However, the recent war in May 2021 with Gaza demonstrated the reality of life here and the fact that many of our surrounding Arab neighbors are not truly interested in seeing a Jewish homeland in their midst. I felt profoundly sad to see the resulting violence in Israel between Arabs and Jews and all around the world as a byproduct of this recent conflagration. It is my premise that the Israel Defense Forces have to exist for our survival. It is not within the concept of "might is right," but that "might" is necessary for us to survive. There is a Hebrew phrase from the Bible that says, "If I am not for myself, then who is for me? And being only for myself, what am I? And if not now, then when?"

However, I believe Israel has to compromise some of its attitudes and laws in order to ensure that our Arab citizens receive equal rights and benefits while still reflecting the fact that we are a Jewish state.

The fact that I live in Haifa has colored many aspects of my life. This is a beautiful city perched on the Carmel mountain range overlooking the Mediterranean Sea, which I can see from my balcony. It is known for its peaceful coexistence with our close and intermingled Arab neighbors. Jerusalem is known for its spiritual essence and culturally mixed population and deserves its distinction as the historic capital of Israel. Tel Aviv is the vibrant cosmopolitan hub of Israel, known for its draw to liberal-minded society, nightlife, culture, high tech, and secular and young Israelis. I like to visit these two other large cities in addition to other beautiful sites throughout our country, but I am very happy to call beautiful, straitlaced, and peaceful Haifa my home.

By working at IBM, first located in the High Tech park next to the beach, and later located on the campus of Haifa University overlooking Haifa Bay and the Carmel National Park, I was truly existing in a prestigious ivory tower. My work and my home on the Carmel isolated me for thirty-one years. I was working and socializing with an elite strata of the population. Not until I retired from IBM and began a new job as a fundraiser for the Haifa Hotline for Domestic Abuse and Children at Risk did I come in contact with and appreciate the full spectrum of the Israeli population. I was working with social workers and psychologists who were Arab (both Christian and Muslim), Russian, Druze, Ethiopian, and Jewish.

It was very enlightening and enriching for me to get to know my coworkers as people I liked and respected.

Meanwhile, my home life was evolving as well. Our children, who were ages two, seven, and nine when we arrived, were becoming true Israelis without receiving any Hebrew, cultural, or homework assistance from my husband or me. The kids became proficient in the language while laughing at, or being embarrassed by, our Hebrew mistakes and accents. They are more comfortable speaking Hebrew at work and at home with their families. But they have continued to converse with me in English. Our son today is a senior project manager at Google. Our oldest daughter is a private psychodrama therapist and supervisor of therapists in special education. She also teaches at Haifa University and Oranim Teachers' College. Our younger daughter is a psychotherapist in her own clinic, as well as in the government welfare sector and for Holocaust survivors. With our progeny to date, the Roth family has increased the Israeli population by fourteen souls.

Politics is a subject that we tended to avoid at home. My husband was very right-wing, feeling that Israel has to be strong and look out for itself, and that we have to preserve our Jewish state at any cost. Even though I understood the logic of his beliefs, I could not go all the way along with his political commitments. I am more of a centrist leaning left, while my children and their spouses are all very leftist. I believe that the Palestinians should eventually have their own state, but we cannot commit to such a move within Israel until they will accept our right to exist and have their own strong and true leaders opposed to terror and committed to peace.

I feel that Israel has changed in many ways concerning the basic values and idealism that existed when we arrived fifty years ago. It was a simpler life then, without financial affluence and exposure to the material accoutrements of the good life elsewhere.

This country is truly a melting pot of people and cultures from all over the world. From being harmonious and idealistic in its principles, it has seemed to splinter, with less tolerance for differing views and observances and political beliefs. This intolerance may be indicative of the discourse and disunity at this time all over the world, but it is very discouraging and revolting to see here.

Even with some of my negative assessments concerning this country, I take great pride in the accomplishments and basic ideals of the Israeli people. Even though there may be dissension among the different groups of the population politically, religiously, ethnically, and economically, they come together and provide support and sustenance in times of need and disaster in Israel and abroad. I am also very proud of the many innovations in various and widespread areas developed here and shared all over the world.

As far as my own personal story is concerned, I am still leading a full life of activity and fulfillment here in Israel. This is my home. I honor my past as an American, and I am proud to be an Israeli. I am content, healthy, and active. I have a very close and loving relationship with my family and warm contacts with friends here and abroad. My continuing volunteer work with the Holocaust survivors as well as at the hospital where my husband was treated gives me great satisfaction.

Besides playing tennis and going to Pilates, my mind stays active with creative writing, copious reading and membership in a book club, subscription to the theater, and participation in a Brainspa -- a program to exercise my cognitive skills. My new and renewed contact with my former Central High School classmates while preparing this collection of life stories has now brought another enrichment to my life.

And recently, a very close relationship with a friend named Ami, whom I met more than thirty years ago at work, metamorphosed into a true love affair and partnership. I had been living alone for more than ten years since becoming widowed. Never did I imagine the pleasure I would derive from living with another person again. He and I are both people pleasers and thrive on this mutual sharing in our everyday lives -- full of much laughter, passion, and contentment. It is fulfilling just to have each other's company and to feel happy and young again. I am learning to take life much easier, with less regimen and with true appreciation for the benefits of this loving relationship on a daily basis.

We do not feel burdened by the usual concerns of existence from when we were maturing and raising our families. We respect each other's individual independence but are assured of each other's dependability as well. Fortunately, at this stage in our shared lives, our families are secure and don't need our constant support and intervention. But we still both reap the satisfaction of continuing love and contact with our respective children and grandchildren.

There is no guarantee of the length of our future together, but in the meantime, day-to-day, we are grateful that we get to enjoy this late-life honeymoon. For sure, being eighty years old (Ami is only seventy-three!) is not the termination of a full life. It is only the beginning of a new chapter. We think our love story demonstrates there is hope for everyone, and that life is full of possibility, no matter how old you are.

Freyda Tresan Roth, Haifa, 2022

Seventy-fifth birthday with family, 2016

10 - Andrea Spruell Kirby

1970s - Breaking Into the All-Male World of Sports TV

In 1971, in Sarasota, Florida, a start-up television station was going on the air. I had talked my way into the job of sportscaster. It was something few, if any, women had ever dared to do: invade the all-male culture of television sports.

My body was shaking all over as I waited to step in front of the camera. After a commercial, the cameraman cued me, and I spoke my first words. "Hello, I'm Andrea Kirby." Then, I delivered the day's sports news as if my presence was no big deal. Little did I know that the phone at the front desk had begun ringing the minute I appeared. Some viewers protested and a few were complimentary, but mostly they were confused. Fortunately, I couldn't hear any of it in the studio. I had just begun my dream.

Whatever effect I was having on viewers, I welcomed it. I could prove I belonged there. The station owner fielded some of the calls coming in and defended me to a vocal audience. Male sportscasters in Tampa and

St. Petersburg gave their theories about me to the media. "People tend not to believe a girl when it comes to sports," said one. "It's a clever gimmick, though." Another said, "We were looking for a girl to do part-time, but we got a good man and gave up the idea."

One night, on my way out of the building after the 11 pm show, I answered the phone myself. The male viewer didn't identify himself, but he was blunt. "You have no business doing a man's job," he said. The comment stung. Until then, I had denied that men, who held all the sports jobs as if this were a male birthright, would object to me. Happily, after two months, I was a fixture to the audience, if still a novelty. I was living my dream.

Sort of. My salary was below a living wage, and I paid my out-of-pocket expenses, such as gasoline for traveling to stories. There was no such thing as overtime pay, and if I had an assignment out of town that went late, I napped in the back of my car. Even that didn't bother me. I was breaking ground. As far as I knew, I was the rare woman broadcasting sports anywhere in the country. Nothing about it discouraged me. Even the colleague who objected to my face.

Craig Sager had accepted the job of cameraman after applying for the sports job that I got. I didn't know this, or him, until he stopped by my desk. "You don't belong here," he said and walked away. I didn't react, but I tried to avoid him after that. Unfortunately, he was assigned to film a promotional tennis event in which I was playing. His film of the match was supposed to air on my show that night. I saw him on the sideline with a camera, although he stayed clear of me, not acknowledging I was part of his assignment. Back at the station, he approached my desk. "Sorry, no film," he said. "The camera wasn't working." A smirk slipped onto his face as he walked away.

The 1970s were open season for harassment, inequality, and discrimination against women. The perpetrators never faced consequences, and women had no choice but to move on without saying a word. This was what I did for most of my career. Sager went on to be a sportscaster at

CNN with no outward evidence he'd changed his opinion about women in sports. Other colleagues at WXLT were my encouragers. Their support made up for the detractors, and I kept improving at my chosen career.

Against the odds, in 1977, four years after my first day as a sportscaster, I landed at the top national network in all of sports broadcasting. No woman had been there before. As a reporter for ABC's Wide World of Sports, I covered events which previously had little television coverage, including auto racing, gymnastics, waterskiing, bowling, and even Mexican cliff diving. Every Saturday in the fall, I was the cohost of College Football Scoreboard. Later, unexpectedly, I was picked to fill in for announcer Frank Gifford, as the ABC Sports Weekend studio anchor. That meant I anchored live, and alone, for two hours. To ABC audiences, I happened overnight, when, in fact, it had been a long road to get there.

The year before I started college at the University of Alabama, Paul "Bear" Bryant became Alabama's head football coach. Until then, Bama's football games were lame social events where students dressed up to watch each other, because the football wasn't worth watching. By Bryant's second year, the team was winning, and the stadium was packed every Saturday. My dorm room looked out on the football practice field, where he stood atop a tall wooden tower watching over practice of the soon-to-be champions. Being able to see football practice from my window made me the envy of the dorm. By 1961, Bryant's third year, Alabama won the college national championship, and the Crimson Tide became the crown jewel in a Deep South state that the rest of the country called backward and racist. Racial trouble at the university started before I arrived and continued after I left. But insulated at what was still an all-white university, I hardly noticed the racial landscape changing around me.

When I discovered the radio and television department at Alabama, I immediately switched my major. Football had a spell over me, and television intrigued me. As a junior at Alabama in 1961 following a football practice, I put the two together for my first sports interview. Parking near

Thomas Field was impossible, so I parked two blocks away and lugged the huge camera tripod with me. I would go back to the car for the camera and the film magazine. Writers were already lined up outside the field waiting for the coach as he walked off. At first, I was quiet, watching others alternate in asking the coach questions, which he answered slowly in a deep, Southern drawl. At a lull, I spoke up, naming my campus station affiliation. Bryant acknowledged me, expecting a question. Instead, I said, "Coach, I have to go to my car for my equipment. You keep going with the others. I'll be right back." I hurried off.

When I returned lugging the 25-pound camera and a 10-pound film canister to where the crowd had been around Bryant, most of the writers had left. But the coach was still there. He watched quietly as I struggled to set up the awkward tripod, lifted the heavy camera and mounted the film magazine on top, locking both down. I unwound the microphone cord, hurried next to him, and leaned into the camera to press the record button. I asked a dozen amateurish questions, and he answered them all. After I finished and thanked him, the future legend left, surrounded by the Alabama Highway Patrol like a school of fish around a great white shark. I was hooked. It felt as natural as anything I had done in my life. That feeling never left me.

I often wondered why Bryant was so accommodating that day. Tough as nails, rigid as steel with players, Bryant insisted on Herculean effort from everyone. After reading *Coach: The Life of Paul "Bear" Bryant* by Keith Dunnavant, I understood. I believe Bryant recognized that I was busting my butt, and a woman working against the odds.

After graduating from college in 1963, I returned to Memphis, where I had gone to high school. Memphis is also where, just a week before I left for my senior year of college, I was with my mom as she died of a stroke. This was my first time in Memphis alone, at twenty-two. And it was where I first worked in radio, although not in sports, and acted in local theater. In Memphis, I also fell in love and married Charlie Kirby, a medical student.

For me, being married was a luxurious return to family and relationships. I didn't mind putting my own dreams on hold for him.

A year later, we settled in Atlanta for his residency at Emory Hospital. Then, like a siren, television called me back, to an entry-level job at the number one station in Atlanta, WSB-TV. Tom Brokaw, a twenty-five-year-old, anchored the news there on his way to becoming an award-winning journalist and the anchor of NBC Nightly News. I had not seen a female counterpart to Brokaw on primetime news. But Brokaw and I were the same age, both from a small town, and, for now, we worked at the same station. I thought this qualified me for a similar future.

Eighteen months later, in 1967, I changed jobs to a less-established station in Atlanta where I talked my way into my first on-air job, giving the noon weather. The station's male weather person was the "weather man," but I was called the "weather girl." The sexist language of the 1960s alluded to my gender as if it were a tolerated disability. Women were allowed to be weather girls across the country, but, to my knowledge, not sports anchors.

That job led to a permanent weather spot on the station's prime-time nightly news. I was certain this would guarantee my future on the air, even if not yet in sports, which is why I didn't mention I was three months pregnant. Pregnant women on television were taboo in the 1960s, so when my condition became obvious, the station tried to hide it. Tighter camera shots made the map harder to see, and by eight months, a work-around was no longer physically possible. I relinquished this golden opportunity, reluctantly.

After baby girl Caroline was born, husband Charlie and I moved to Florida, where he joined a medical practice and I settled into being a stay-at-home mom. I jogged, played tennis and racquetball, and soon gave birth to our son, Gentry. I hardly noticed that I still had television dreams on hold. Heartbreakingly, when the kids were two years and four years old, our marriage ended in divorce. We were immature with childish expectations that had eroded our relationship through a thousand cuts. As a single mother with two kids, I needed a job.

An article in the local newspaper announced the launch of that new television station in Sarasota. I called to audition for the weather job, but when the owner said the weather position was filled, I didn't miss a beat. "That's fine," I said. "What I really want to do is sports."

Even in small market Sarasota, I was able to cover several Major League Baseball teams that came to Florida every year for spring training. I learned the sport from players, writers, coaches, and managers. But as the only person in the station's sports department, I worked overtime, while juggling motherhood alone. I was usually exhausted, and one night, I began to stutter on the air. A well-known sports figure was retiring, and when I got to the word "retire," I couldn't say it. Only a hum came out as if my tongue was stuck to the roof of my mouth. I tried to relax, but inside I panicked. Looking down at the copy, I was mute. The studio was hushed except for the buzz coming from a klieg light overhead. The cameraman leaned out to look at me. The weather person was fidgeting off camera. My face flushed, and I thought I might faint. I stopped trying to speak, forcing myself to relax during the endless, humiliating quiet. As quickly as I had plummeted down this hole, I snapped out of it and finished the segment.

I was shaken. For two weeks I avoided words that started with r and v, which made my writing sound very odd. I worked through it, but I knew the stutter could return at any time. Eventually, I was myself again, doing what I loved. Sports had always gotten me through tough times. And football was still my favorite.

As a kid growing up in Alabama, I tagged along to high school football games with my older siblings. Playing underneath the spectator stands with other kids, the sounds of crashing of bodies on the field and cheering in the stands became the soundtrack of my early life. Football felt like home.

My childhood hometown, Russellville, Alabama, was nearly unnoticeable on a map, tucked in the northwest corner of the state near the border of Mississippi and Tennessee, blanketed with pine trees. To describe my childhood as free-range in the 1940s would be redundant. Every child ran free if so inclined. Outside from sunup to sundown, I had no adult supervision or rules that I recall. Infrequent friends were tomboys like I was, but they lived in town while I lived farther out. They weren't as interested in being outside as I was, plus, they had more convenient playmates. Mostly, I was alone.

My dad, Hugh Spruell, and my mom, Lucille Claiborne, moved to Russellville from Memphis, after my father graduated from medical school with specialties in family medicine and surgery. Often when his patients were unable to pay for his services, he accepted baked goods and livestock, instead. He had built a barn and paddock specifically for these animals. My parents convinced each of their four children that we were smart, talented, and capable of anything. I didn't know what that meant, but the way they said it made me feel good.

At dinnertime, we gathered in a commotion with my dad at the head of the table, still wearing his three-piece suit that smelled like the hospital. He told stories about his patients, embellishing the details for laughs. In the overlapping chatter, there was hardly a table manner in sight. Martha Ann, the oldest, and Nancy, the second girl, were the loudest. My brother Hugh, two years older than I, always drowned me out. I had plenty to say, but as the youngest, I seldom got the chance to say it.

My dad had left for World War II by the time I was two years old. Serving as a flight surgeon, he once parachuted into the Burmese jungle to treat wounded soldiers. I was five when he came home, and soon after that my parents were divorced. They didn't meet with us to talk about what divorce meant for us kids, and I seemed to be the only one who was upset. Our mom was moving to Memphis without us. I didn't understand. We visited her, of course, but that wasn't enough. I needed my mom.

Our dad threw money at his guilt over the divorce. He had a tennis court built, which no one knew how to use, and a swimming pool with two diving boards. The day the pool was completed and filled with water, Daddy came to find me in the barn. "Come on, Chicken," he said. "Time to learn to swim." Chicken was his affectionate name for me. Smiling as we walked toward the pool, I wondered why he was still in his street clothes. How was he going in the pool without swim trunks? Soon, I realized he wasn't going in at all. At the edge of the pool, he grabbed me up under both arms and tossed me into the pool. I plunged three feet under the water. Shocked, I thrashed to the surface, but slipped under again, and again. I could only keep my head above water for a few seconds, but in one of those moments I saw a watery version of him on the side of the pool. He didn't look worried, at all, in fact he was smiling. Then he shouted, "Swim, Chicken!"

Fear, adrenaline, and thrashing finally propelled me to the side of the pool where he pulled me out, chuckling. This was how my father conducted life, as if success was only a matter of certainty and action. He taught me to live fearlessly.

Suddenly a swimmer, I would drag a solid, heavy metal deck chair to the side of the pool where I pushed it in and jumped in after it. I was there many days, mostly alone, at the bottom of the pool with one arm anchoring me down to the chair. I came up often for air but returned to the chair where I spent hours. Surrounded by the silence of deep water, I played out imaginary scenes. Pretending to smoke, I told fascinating stories to a captive audience. I was practicing for when I was an adult with something to say.

When I was ten, my father's small plane crashed in a field outside the dirt strip of Russellville's airport. He had been taking Boy Scouts up for "joy" rides, which included a nose-down spin toward the ground to make the ride exciting. A thirteen-year-old Boy Scout died along with my dad that day. My dad was forty-five years old. I was ten.

The day after the funeral, our mom drove to Russellville to take us to Memphis to live with her. I was up early to ride my horse for the last time. Then, in the pool, I swam back and forth like an agitated goldfish. I dove under, again and again, crying underwater and choking in the process. I skimmed my torso along the concrete bottom as if I could scrape this memory into my skin. I couldn't imagine life without my horse, the open spaces, or the pool.

Mom's car crunched down the gravel driveway, away from the big house forever as I curled up next to the warm glass of the backseat window and watched my childhood disappear. My parents had insisted I could do anything -- except stay there.

Memphis was as foreign to me as a different country would have been, and mom's 1,400-square-foot house was claustrophobic. I escaped on roller skates to city sidewalks that let me glide for blocks without stopping, until dark. Neighborhood girls invited me to play inside, once. Gathered around an obscene number of dolls and creating imaginary dialogue for them was torture. I returned to my skates, and the endless sidewalks.

School was another place where I was an outsider. The kids in junior high had all been together since grammar school and saw no need to add me to their social circle. By the time I got to Central High School, things were better. Students and teachers supported the school's football team like fanatics. I became part of that fan group by default. Intramural basketball was the only sport for girls, so I played that, and took fencing and trampoline at the YMCA. I was voted Most Athletic by my classmates my senior year. As it had before and would in the future, my interest in sports got me through some tough years.

Sports also took me and my kids to several cities across the country. From my first sports job in Sarasota, I landed in Baltimore, where I was introduced to the local sports fans at a Colts game when a small prop plane buzzed over the stadium, trailing a banner that read:

WJZ-TV Channel 13

Andrea Kirby Knows Baltimore Sports!

Hardly. I had a lot of catching up to do, while the station's veteran sports personality, Nick Charles, already had a loyal following in the market.

At one Orioles game, Curt Motton, a reserve outfielder, approached me without introduction or preamble. "Lady, do you know what an ERA is?" I replied, "Yes, Curt -- Earned Run Average." I didn't say, "I also know what your batting average is .145, which is why you don't play." Most of the athletes were accepting, cooperative, and friendly. If they objected to me, they kept it to themselves. It was male staff and broadcasters who objected openly. A veteran cameraman at WJZ was one of the objectors. Working with him could make my day very long. On assignment, he was rude and uncooperative, and once he even failed to deliver the shots I needed for the story. Then he blurted out, "You have no business in this job."

Nick Charles, the sports director, also took my presence personally. He was dismissive and sarcastic, and once, he punched a hole in the sheet-rock of our shared office, stormed out to the newsroom, and announced I was fired. Nick didn't have the power to fire me, so we were both back at work the next day. But not long after that, Nick left WJZ for a job in another city, and ultimately became a star on CNN Sports.

Everyone expected I would be promoted to his job when he left. I was popular in the market and drew consistently high ratings from sports viewers. Nevertheless, a man was hired to replace Nick. Station management had encouraged everything I did over the years. It was the parent company, Westinghouse, that lacked the foresight to make the gutsy move -- the right move -- to promote me. Even an insult as blatant as this one couldn't shake my belief that I was on the right path.

Within weeks, ABC Sports called me to audition with the network. The auditions went even better than I hoped, and I signed a three-year contract. At that moment, every lingering disappointment evaporated. I began to have constant dreams of flying -- not on an airplane, but with my own two arms, on a gentle breeze, in a blue sky, like a superhero.

One of the first events I covered on Wide World of Sports was the Women's Primo Masters surfing competition on the North Shore of Oahu, Hawaii. I arrived a day early to film my on-camera open, in which I would ride a surfboard for the show's opening. I had to stay on the board for only fifteen seconds, but after I fell off several times, my coach, surfing champion Fred Hemmings, took me out farther, where a bigger wave could easily get under the board. "Time to try this for the camera." Fred said.

It was a tentative ride, but I managed to stay up on the board for fifteen seconds, enough for the opening segment. What viewers didn't see was right after that fifteen-second ride, when I was knocked off and sucked under by the undertow of incoming waves a few times. I was sure I would die. Instead, I spent the night at the hotel throwing up. The next afternoon, I was standing at Haleiwa Beach to cover the women's surfing competition. Fred Hemmings stood beside me. Wearing a bright green swimsuit, I giggled to myself that this was my work uniform. This dream was so bright I needed shades.

My reporting assignments for Wide World of Sports took me to exotic places: Germany for horse jumping, Sweden for cross country skiing, and Lake Como, Italy for a waterskiing competition. I also co-anchored College Football Scoreboard, the only place fans could get the scores of Saturday games across the country. I was flying high, which is why the call I got from network executives, two-and-a-half years into my three-year contract with ABC, surprised me.

The network had decided not to renew my contract. I didn't see it coming and I felt betrayed. ABC had chosen me thoughtfully, only to give up on me before the end of my contract. I couldn't recall signs that would have warned me something was wrong. "Good job," was the only feedback I'd received for two-and-a-half years. Then, suddenly, "You're fired." I was never asked how I could best contribute to the network, and I never had a seat at the table with decision-makers, all of them men. I wanted to be more than the first woman, I wanted to be good, to be a valuable broadcaster. I never recognized the implicit, impenetrable glass ceiling that was always there for me as a woman.

After I left ABC, my dream morphed into a time of survival. From 1979 to 1984, I had no steady job but learned to be a freelance broadcaster. It was unpredictable, but more interesting than I expected. Cohosting the Soviet National Games in Moscow was life changing. And, I called play-by-play for women's tennis on USA Network alongside former tennis player Mary Carillo. In 1980, I signed a contract for regular hosting work on a live morning talk show, Good Morning New York, with cohost Spencer Christian. Live television was my happy place, doing interviews was my next favorite. So, I was excited about this new challenge. Even the hours suited me. I arrived at the studio at 7 am and was home by 3 pm, giving me more time with Caroline and Gentry, both in school in a suburb of New York City.

After six months, Good Morning New York was losing in the ratings to The Phil Donahue Show, as it was when Spencer and I got there. Our show producer became paranoid and distant, then the atmosphere in the building became toxic as everyone sensed we were in trouble. Chuck Gingold, the program director, called me in to soften me for an end that I found out later was already in the works. He quoted the research they had done: "Successful talk shows," he said, "never have a female cohost who is dominant."

Immediately after that, the format of the show changed to make Spencer appear to be the lead host, while I was told to "tamp down" my personality, and to defer to Spencer. This unnatural behavior was painful for me. I practically disappeared on the show. Then, Spencer and I were subjected to a focus group to let audiences decide what to do with the show -- meaning me. Spencer had a three-year contract with no option. He wasn't going anywhere. My contract had an option that allowed WABC to release me after one year.

Initially, Gingold had told me viewers found me "real" and "likable." Three months after asking me to change my personality, I was only "sort of likable." Then, he delivered the final blow. "Frankly, Andrea," he said, "we don't feel you're strong enough." Too strong or not strong enough, I wasn't going to win this battle. Sexism was sometimes subtle, more often overt, and usually career-killing. I was let go.

Once again, I needed a job. Part-time weekend work at New York's WNEW-TV in a small pool of reporters seemed reliable. One weekend, on a Giants' game assignment, I headed to the locker room after the game with the rest of the media. The guard at the door stopped me. "Sorry," he said, "women aren't allowed in the locker room." No problem. I adapted. The team's media person would bring players out to me, where I interviewed them in the hallway. A TV interview in a dark hallway is no substitute for the locker room with players still full of emotion, heartbreak, or joy. The next time I covered a Giants game, coach Bill Parcells was brought to me in the hallway, but he showed up too late for me to finish the story in time for the nightly show. WNEW never assigned me to another Giants game. That cost me several Sundays of the microscopic pay on which I depended.

Thankfully, the Jets had no such policy. But I made sure to stop outside the locker room first, while the cameraman announced I would be entering. We did this strictly as a courtesy. Then, the cameraman would wave me in. As usual, I had to look around for my interview subject, my least favorite task. Once, from the farthest corner of the room, a player not wearing a stitch of clothing began a long, locker room strut past me, at full bounce. Then, a second player walked right up to me, stopping inside my personal space. "You should be ashamed of yourself," he said, "being here where players are undressed." I sensed the cameraman shift in place. "I'm sorry if you feel uncomfortable," I said. "That's not my intent." Then he asked, "Why do you need to be in here?"

I replied, "I'm a reporter. It's not practical for me to wait outside -- players don't want to come out. If I don't get my interview, I don't get paid." He didn't respond, so I continued. "I always ask the cameraman to announce when I'm coming in, so guys have time to get dressed, if they want to. I hope that helps." He walked away. They soon got used to me.

In 1985, on the last day of the Big East basketball tournament at Madison Square Garden, after Georgetown beat Syracuse in the final game, I went for post-game interviews. Georgetown's star center, Patrick Ewing, had never given an interview before, by order of his coach. Now, a scrum of eager sports writers gathered tightly around him. Ewing looked very uncomfortable. His eyes darted above the writers' heads, and he answered in monosyllables. The writers tried to help him, repeating and rephrasing questions for him. Nothing helped. He looked like he might pass out. I was the only television reporter, so I waited until the print reporters had finished to get my on-camera interview. I stepped in front of him as the cameraman positioned his shot over my shoulder. I asked easy questions, hoping Ewing would relax, but he was sweating now, not from exertion, but because he was so uncomfortable in this role.

It was as painful to watch played back on television, as it had been to see in person. But Ewing wasn't the only athlete who reacted this way to media attention. That night, an idea dawned on me: I could teach players how to be better in interviews and at communicating with writers and broadcasters. More ideas came fast. At first, I scribbled on scraps of paper. Next, I filled notebooks with what I would teach players. Then, I knew who I wanted to be my first client.

A few weeks later, in the third inning of a New York Mets game, I left the press box to find Mets general manager Frank Cashen. He had been in Baltimore with the Orioles when I was there with WJZ-TV. Now he was building the Mets into a championship team, and I had something valuable to offer. I stuck my head inside the owner's box where Cashen usually watched the game. Al Harazin, his second in command, was watching alone. He invited me in, and I launched into the Ewing story. Then, I made my pitch. In 1984, the team was on the brink of a championship, and its young players needed help handling the inevitable media crush. "The more the Mets win," I said, "the more coverage they'll get. They must be ready to handle it. Media training will help them stay out of trouble." Harazin ended the discussion with, "I'll talk with Frank and get back to you."

My feet barely touched the ground on the way to my car. I believed Harazin would bring Cashen on board. Three days later, the phone rang. It was Harazin. "Okay, we're in," he said. "When and where do you propose to do this?" I could feel the warm Florida sun already. "Spring Training," I said. "Okay," he said. Harazin never asked what I would teach, or how. The Mets trusted me with valuable young prospects, which was humbling. We settled on a fee, and Harazin agreed without hesitation. I let out a deep breath and got to work planning what I would teach.

I stepped off the plane from New York to the breathtaking feel of the tropical climate, where warm breezes blew palm trees to a soft clicking sound. The meeting room for the first-ever media workshop was a quick walk from the practice field. Out the window, I saw the players headed toward me. Star right fielder Darryl Strawberry led the way, followed closely by Dwight "Doc" Gooden, the Mets nineteen-year-old pitching prospect, then relievers Jesse Orosco and Doug Sisk, and, finally, third baseman Howard Johnson. They were quiet as they came into the room and sized me up. It took a few minutes for the players to negotiate their places at the table as long legs stuck out the front or off to the side. At 5 feet, 5 inches, I needed all the presence I could muster, so I stood for three days. It was just the beginning of my new dream.

I found media coaching unpredictable but thoroughly satisfying. As a middle-aged woman with no athletic achievement, I was a different kind of coach, and ours was a unique relationship. Through two decades, I coached almost every major league baseball team, multiple NFL, NHL, and NBA teams, and was the broadcast coach for ESPN. Other clients followed: golfers, a spokesman for bass fishing, famous model Niki Taylor, and eighteen teams competing in the 1996 Olympic Games. The first women I coached were LPGA professional golfers, and professional tennis players with the WTA. Coaching women was unlike coaching men. With boundless energy, they were eager, intense, and appreciative of the attention. They challenged me without hesitation. All of this role fit me like a glove.

That day in 1971, in Sarasota, when I first stepped in front of the television camera to introduce myself as an unlikely sportscaster, I was sure that it was only the start of a long, on-air career. A decade later, a twenty-one-year-old college basketball star inspired me to a new dream. I didn't understand it at the time. But I never doubted I could do any of it. Because I always remembered my dad's words, propelling me to fearlessness: "Swim, Chicken."

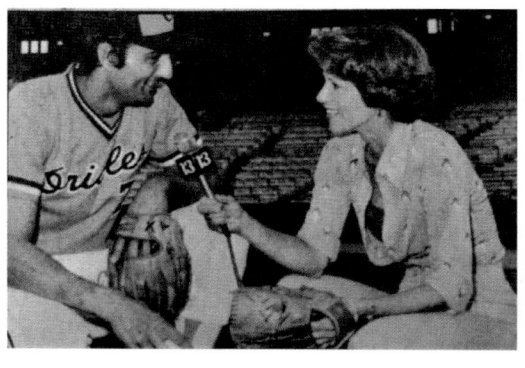 

Interviewing Orioles Mark Belanger, Baltimore, 1974   Andrea Spruell Kirby, 2017

This story is a condensed version of a book by Andrea Kirby, about her time as a sportscaster and sports media coach.

11 - Milt Masson

1980s - The Reagan and Bush Years

In 1949, when I was eight years old, a girl named Jane Elizabeth Teas and her family moved in, two doors down from my family. Little did I know then that we would start dating in ninth grade, and that Jane would be not only my first love, but my only love, and she would become my wife and the love of my life.

Thirty years later, in 1979, Jane, our two kids, and I were living in Phoenix, Arizona. I was a partner in my own engineering firm and had become active in Republican politics. That's when I joined Ronald Reagan's presidential campaign team as the Western Political Director. After his 1980 election victory, I then became part of his transition team, in charge of presidential personnel for the Western states. When he took office in 1981, I received two presidential appointments -- to the board of the congressionally chartered U.S. Synthetics Fuels Corporation, and to the board of the U.S. Legal Services Corporation. But I missed my family and Arizona and soon returned to Phoenix, working to further expand my engineering firm.

In 1984, I hit the campaign trail again, to help re-elect Reagan for a second term. After I attended the second inauguration with Jane and the kids, Vice President George H. W. Bush invited me to join him for a fishing trip on the middle fork of the Salmon River in Idaho. That was a great experience. It led me to return to the political arena in 1987, serving as the Western campaign manager for Bush's presidential run.

After his victory in 1988, I took Jane and the kids to the inaugural events, where they had the opportunity to spend some quality time alone with George and Barbara Bush. That was the full run of my national political career. In 1988, we returned home to Arizona, and I had no further involvement in political campaigns.

Looking back, the days at Central were such a pivotal time in my life. My political interest began during the Eisenhower administration. But my teachers at Central further encouraged and inspired my public service, always emphasizing the importance of participation in public life.

High school was also the time when I became serious in my growing love for Jane. We did not have all the distractions of this day and time, nor the instant and constant news of the hour. Consequently, we spent more time with family, friends, and school activities. Memphis was a small old southern town in the Bible Belt, and church was a big part of my growing up. Central was the first high school in Memphis. It was in the center of our Midtown neighborhood, where most of us were within walking distance to school. As we were growing up, we gathered many afternoons after school for ice cream at Stoke's Drug and played games like Cowboys and Indians around our neighborhood.

Music was a huge part of my childhood, too. When I was five, my mother started my piano lessons while I attended Miss Lee's Kindergarten. I continued with piano all the way through my first year in college. I started playing the trombone at Bellevue Junior High and continued to play it in the band at Central High School. During high school, I practiced piano for at least an hour a day and many days for more than two hours. By the time I gave my high school certificate recital, I was getting burned out on classical piano. Then, I was accepted at North Texas State College on a piano scholarship. That's where I fell in love with jazz music. Jazz has remained a major interest throughout my life. At North Texas, several friends and I formed a small jazz group and played mostly for fun or at an occasional small event.

During my first year at North Texas, my father developed terminal cancer. I also missed Jane, who was on a scholarship to Ole Miss. That's when my cousin Jim Ellers, the founder of Ellers and Reaves Engineering, offered me a job as draftsman if I came home and studied engineering at Christian Brothers College in Memphis. I had become very interested in math and physics, so it sounded like the best move. I graduated from Christian Brothers in 1964, with a degree in electrical engineering, and continued to work at Ellers Engineering. Jane was very active in Phi Mu sorority and graduated college after only three years. So, before I finished college, we got married on June 8, 1963, at LaBelle Haven Baptist Church in Olive Branch, Mississippi, near Memphis.

We purchased our first home in Raleigh, just outside of Memphis, and I took a job after graduation with the chemical division of Quaker Qats in Memphis, as the Director of Engineering and Maintenance for the electrical department. We became active in Central Christian Church, where I sang in choir. Jane taught fifth grade, I joined the Memphis Engineers Club, and we purchased a ski boat which we took to Pickwick Lake every chance we had. In 1966, I accepted an offer to join Westinghouse Electric in Kansas City. So, our journey west began.

For two years we enjoyed the culture of Kansas City, but the winters were cold with lots of snow. While I was shoveling snow one Saturday, my cousin Jim in Memphis called and asked me to consider opening a branch engineering office of his Memphis firm out west in Reno, Nevada. He assured me that soon after that, I could move with the family to Phoenix, where he had another office, and where it was much warmer than winters in Kansas City.

That is how we ended up moving to Arizona in 1968. And almost immediately after we arrived, we began our family -- first with a daughter, Michelle, soon followed by a son, Craig. Then, we designed and built a home in Phoenix, and I decided to help build our own large regional engineering, architectural, and construction management firm: Sullivan and Masson. We grew and opened offices in Las Vegas, Palo Alto, Tucson, and Washington, DC, specializing in design of hotels, hospitals, AT&T facilities, and college dormitories.

The first person I met the week we moved to Phoenix was Jack Smithbaker. He became my best friend and good business associate. Jack had a twin Comanche airplane and a great fishing boat in San Carlos, Mexico, which we enjoyed on many fun trips with our wives. Jack and I took several fishing trips to Baja Mexico, sometimes landing his airplane right on the beach. Jack was a founding member of the Fiesta Bowl Committee, active in the community, and a leader in Western Republican politics. That's how and when I first got involved.

In the 1960s we were a much smaller political community. We all knew each other, there were fewer lobbyists, and much less media focus on politics. The politicians of both parties were able to work together to get things done without a lot of turmoil. They would often end their day together with drinks or dinner. I remember flying home from DC sitting next to Democratic Senator Tip O'Neill, who encouraged me to stay active in politics. He said, "We need good people active on both sides of the aisle." Tip was one of the best, most honest and effective legislators in Washington.

In 1976, after having worked on Ronald Reagan's first unsuccessful run for president, I helped start the Western States Political Caucus. Our goal was to organize all the western states which had small populations and large land mass in common compared with the more heavily populated states in the remainder of the country. That meant we didn't include

California, since it was the largest state in the country. We worked to convince Congress not to distribute funds for infrastructure, such as highways and utilities, based on population alone, as that would discriminate against these larger, less populated states in the West. We were successful in helping make this happen. In 1979, we converted this to a Reagan for President organization.

As we entered the Reagan era in 1980, the two parties became more polarized, thus making compromise much more difficult. Big business, through their lobbyists, began to exercise more power and influence. Throughout the Reagan years the power of the corporate lobbyists continued to gain more influence.

After my time in politics, I concentrated on growing my engineering firm and enjoying my family. We quickly grew to become one of the largest consulting engineering firms in the West.

In the later 1980s, I became a founding member and second president of the board of the Arizona State Chamber of Commerce. I also served on the Arizona Safe Roads Committee, Phoenix Men's Symphony Guild, and Arizona Professional Engineers Club. Jane and I often took the kids to Utah, where they learned to snow ski. Michelle became a champion swimmer, and Craig succeeded in playing sports. We outgrew our house and moved to a larger home in Paradise Valley, a suburb of Phoenix.

Our entire family became active in church and were founding members at Chaparral Christian Church, a nondenominational church in Scottsdale. I sang in the choir, Jane taught Sunday school, and I was an elder.

Jane became very active with the Phoenix Zoo, served on the board of the Phoenix Zoo Auxiliary, and traveled to almost every zoo in the country looking at exhibits and bringing home ideas. I often got to go along with her. We even traveled to Churchill, Canada, with a group of her zoo friends to watch the polar bears prepare to spend the winter on the polar ice as it began to freeze. We stayed in trailers mounted on stilts above the frozen tundra so that it would not melt. While there we went out in large buses with enormous tires on the frozen tundra to watch the bears as they would often approach our vehicle and peer through the windows. We took a dogsled ride one day to watch the bears approach the ice and took a helicopter ride the following day to see the bears running along the edge of the ice at full speed.

In the 2000s, I retired and my engineering firm dissolved. But my son Craig and I, and John Ellers, the son of my cousin Jim Ellers who was so pivotal in my career and my life, formed PolyTek Rubber and Recycling. It rapidly became one of the largest tire recycling and crumb rubber manufacturing companies in the United States. With five plants around the country, we were able to recycle a vast number of scrap tires and became a leader in the development of the use of crumb rubber in asphalt and playgrounds.

During these years I remained active on local boards, was an elder at church, and sang in church and community choirs. Jane remained active in Zoo Auxiliary and taught Sunday School. Michelle and Craig were growing up and both soon married, with wedding ceremonies in our backyard in Scottsdale. In 2003, I also formed the Masson Company, to provide consulting services to companies seeking assistance in preparing business plans and obtaining financing.

Everything was going well until 2013, when Jane became ill and was diagnosed with non-small cell lung cancer. Less than 10 percent who have it have never smoked. Jane smoked one cigarette in high school, did not like it, and never smoked another one. Knowing the odds and trying to live somewhat of a normal life, she underwent both chemo and radiation. We celebrated our fiftieth wedding anniversary on June 8, 2018 at my son's home. More than 150 friends and family attended, with quite a few coming from out of town. During the coming weeks we enjoyed every moment together and went to several museums and the zoo.

Soon, Jane took a turn for the worse, developed pneumonia, and passed away only four days later. My cousin Jim's son John and I stayed twenty-four hours a day at her bedside in the hospital those last few days. I held her hand saying the Lord's prayer as she took her last breath. Immediately after I said "Amen," she loosened her grip on my hand and passed into the Lord's hands.

As I left the hospital, it seemed like I was in a dream waiting for it to pass and spent several days in a state of shock. That led to a period of deep depression which lasted for a couple of years. I attended grief counseling sessions several times a week until my grief counselor passed away. All this time, I remained active in church and choir but was not ready to get back to being involved with any professional activities. I finally woke up one morning and decided to face reality as of today -- not yesterday -- not tomorrow. I reconnected with a few consultant clients, started exercising every day, lost more than 100 pounds, and began to crawl out from under my rock.

Here is part of a poem I wrote during that time.

Trying today to not think of battles to fight, nor of battles already fought,

But rather to focus on the now and how I will live in today.

It sounds so easy but in truth is so tough to do.

For without Jane always at my side it is hard in every way

As now is blurred by grief and the future uncertain too.

I pray to God for answers, for guidance, and strength to endure

The days ahead and the challenges to be faced.

I grew up in Memphis surrounded by a very large family, then went off to college in Texas in 1959, living in a men's dorm with all the freshmen. Then it was back home to Memphis, again living at home. After Jane and I married in 1963, we lived together happily for the next fifty years. Now, for the first time, I am faced, not only with her loss, but also with the inevitability that I am really alone. I am still not sure how to deal with this

-- although keeping busy helps. I can only pray and hope that each new day will slowly bring me to a new sense of purpose and joy of living with help from a few close friends, family, grandkids, and the Good Lord.

While camping in the Dragoon Mountains recently with my son Craig and my grandson Colter for four days, we had none of the usual distractions of TV, internet, emails, telephone, or normal daily activities. Quality time with Craig and Colter was enough. I had time each day in one of the most beautiful places in Arizona to simply sit quietly and think, pray, reflect, and connect with God.

I remain active at Chaparral Christian Church, the church in Scottsdale that our family was a part of founding in the 1980s. Jane is now resting in peace at the church columbarium, where I will be joining her someday. I now look forward to staying active in business, community, and church activities. I know God has a plan for me and I must work diligently each day to identify and fulfill that plan. I also know I have been so blessed, and am still blessed, with a full and rewarding life.

Jane Teas Masson and Milton Masson

Wedding, 1963, Olive Branch, Mississippi   Fiftieth anniversary, 2013, Scottsdale, Arizona

12 - Eddie Felsenthal

1990s - Big Dreams, Big Booms and Busts

In the 1990s, I had a dream. I dreamed that my three sons would move back to Memphis after college and join me in my business. It was just as I had done in 1963, returning to my hometown after college and joining my father's company.

I even envisioned them living in houses that backed up to ours so that their future children could enjoy our big backyard. By then, I had built my father's life insurance business into a successful financial services company that included life insurance, retirement plans, and employee benefits. I had become a founding and life member of the Top of the Table, a group of the highest-producing financial industry leaders from among those who qualify for the industry's Million Dollar Round Table. And I had won the Flagship Award from New England Mutual Life Insurance one year, for being the all-around leading producer. With the help of some wonderful teammates, I also serviced the retirement plans and employee benefit plans of some of the mid-South's leading businesses. Life was good.

But in September 1998, my dream turned into a nightmare. To realize my expanding vision, I had developed two additional companies and moved the entire operation to a building I had renovated on Shelby Oaks Drive in Memphis. While living in my dream world, I failed to stay grounded in reality.

One of the businesses, a registered investment company, failed after an employee -- who ultimately went to prison -- made and covered up reckless trades that collapsed along with the stock market crash of September 1998. The other business, a property and casualty agency, lost most of its revenue when an employee left, taking with him a large portion of the customer base that we had recently purchased from his father. We had to sell the building on Shelby Oaks Drive to help compensate those who had lost funds in the registered investment company.

I realized then that it was fortunate my sons had not come home to be part of my business. Instead, they had taken the advice given to them by my close friend and former college classmate Lee Taylor to "fly away and do their own thing." My three sons were following their own dreams.

Edward moved to New York and went into journalism, a field he had always loved. He is now the editor-in-chief and CEO of *Time*. Marty moved first to Nashville and then to San Francisco, where he started a venture capital firm, Health Velocity Capital, specializing in healthcare services. David moved to McLean, Virginia, where he first helped run a healthcare company, the Advisory Board, and now is CEO of EAB, an education research technology and data enabled company. As it turned out, their children rarely use our big backyard.

As life went on, I learned more about dreams and about legacies. I had hoped to pass a legacy onto my children and their children, a family business and way of life in a community that has meant so much to my wife, Gloria, and to me. Instead, I realized I had passed on a different kind of legacy, one of embracing the life you build and the path you pave for yourself and others. In Judaism, we call it Shehecheyanu.

I have also realized I come from a long line of dreamers. The dreams of my great-grandparents brought them to the United States in the late 1840s from the little village of Munchweiler, Germany, in the Alsace-Lorraine region. They settled in Brownsville, Tennessee, and in 1883, moved to nearby Jackson, Tennessee, where they reared eight children. My great-grandfather was one of the organizers of the Jewish temple in Jackson. My grandfather, J. C. Felsenthal, later served as president. He also served as an alderman in Jackson and as a member of the school board. My grandmother, Cecilia Felsenthal, served in many civic and temple positions as well. Like many Jews in the South, the two of them sought to assimilate while keeping ties to the Jewish community.

By the early 1900s, many of the male family members were working for the family's J. C. Felsenthal Co. Wholesale Grocers. In January 1926, when my father turned twenty-one and was soon to graduate from Washington and Lee University, his father gave him $10,000 of stock in the family business, and he wrote the following in a letter that I still have today: "My object in the last few years has been to build up a business so that when you are finished with school, you will be able to come into it, and that with the assistance of your brother and uncles can carry on successfully and maintain the name that I have tried to protect from any and all blemish." He continued, "I extend to you with the deepest feeling that a father can express my deepest love and best wishes that you may live to enjoy many, happy, happy years."

Unfortunately, shortly thereafter, when Malone and Hyde, a much larger wholesale grocer based in Memphis, began selling groceries throughout West Tennessee, J. C. Felsenthal Co. could not compete, and Dad helped his father liquidate the business.

But my grandfather's dream lived on in other ways. By 1929, Dad and his brother and parents had moved to Memphis. My father started working with MassMutual Life Insurance company. Ten years later, he moved to New England Mutual Life Insurance Company, because Charles D.

Richardson, an older man with an established position in the community, offered him the position of assistant general agent. This was an unusual opportunity for him. In those days, and even in 1963, when I started in the life insurance business, insurance and financial companies often wanted male Jewish salesmen, but they rarely wanted them as executives or even as general agents. In 1957, like his father before him in 1937, Dad became president of Temple Israel, the Memphis Reform Temple.

My father was thirty-one when he married my mother, Pearl Thalheimer, from Little Rock, Arkansas in 1936. My mom regretted not being able to go to college. Instead, she went to secretarial school, where she learned typing and shorthand. She was twenty-four when she married and moved to Memphis. In 1939, when my grandfather died, my parents moved into my grandmother's house on Belvedere Boulevard in Midtown Memphis. They shared the house with my grandmother and one of my uncles, until he got married. I was born in 1941 and grew up in that house.

My father believed competition was a good teacher for life. He was a champion boxer in college and always encouraged me to participate in competitive sports. But I was no good at baseball, not good enough in basketball, and too small for football. Tennis became my sport. Most of my tennis was limited to playing at either of two public courts in Memphis, or at the city's Jewish country club, Ridgeway Country Club. With very few exceptions, Jewish people and Black people were not invited to be members at any of the city's other country clubs. After college I also had access to the two private courts of the Taylor family at their Wildwood Farm. Every Saturday afternoon, Bill Taylor invited many of the best tennis players in the city to his courts. In 1974, the Racquet Club opened in East Memphis with none of the usual country club religious or racial restrictions on membership.

When my senior year at Central approached, I knew I was expected to follow in my father's footsteps and go to Washington and Lee. But in my own diversion from the path my father dreamed for me, I went to Princeton

University instead. That year, eight of us from Memphis were accepted to the then all-male university. In 1959, the number of Jewish students was limited, and there was only one African American student in my class.

In June 1963, back in sync with my family's dreams, I returned to Memphis to work with my father, who was struggling with terminal lung cancer at age fifty-eight, due to his lifelong smoking habit. I began selling insurance and other financial services, which felt comfortable, after having sold Fuller brushes and office machines in the two previous summers during college.

Dad died the following September. It was hard, but I knew he would be proud that, with the help of my mother, I was able to keep most of his clients after he died. Many of them were older Jewish merchants who became mentors to me as well as clients.

At the time, many of the companies were family oriented. For example, one company included a father and son-in-law. Another company included a father, a son-in-law of the founder, and the founder's son. There was often a son or son-in-law, but never a daughter or daughter-in-law. If the son-in-law happened to get a divorce from the daughter of an owner, the situation became complex. There were few expectations in those days for a daughter to be an active part of a family business, and unfortunately I have no recollection of a daughter-in-law becoming active in a family business among my clients.

Soon after returning home, while working, I enrolled in the night program at the law school at Memphis State University, graduating in 1969. I also added non-Jewish clients to my existing list of clients. In addition, I got many referrals from the law firm of Marvin Ratner and my Central High classmate Irvin Salky. The two of them, along with renowned Black lawyers Russell Sugarmon and A. W. Willis, started the first racially integrated law firm in Memphis and in Tennessee in July of 1967. The firm was a leader in the fight for civil rights in the South.

Through the fifty-eight years I have been in business, I have had some wonderful associates. In 2005, I won a lifetime achievement award from Metropolitan Life Insurance Company for service to clients. But the success of Felsenthal Financial Services is due to the small group of folks who were part of it and still are. David Deaderick, an MBA from the University of Arkansas, joined in 1969. Judy Viar joined in 1988, and Cecilia Watson, CPA, many years later. Imogene Tisdale, now deceased, worked with us for more than forty years. Imogene grew up in Jackson, Tennessee. She raised her family, participated in civic and religious activities, and ran our pension department. Like many women of their generation, neither Imogene nor Judy went to college, and they had limited access to law school or professional degrees. If Judy and Imogene had been born thirty years later, they probably would have run their own companies or professional offices.

When I was thirty-seven, a client of mine who knew tennis star Bobby Riggs set up a match between Riggs and me. Riggs was sixty years old, but he was a former world number one tennis player. I won the first set 7-6, Riggs won the second set 6-2 as well as a $100 bet from my client. And when I was forty-one, I won the City of Memphis Tennis Championships. After that, I retired from my competitive tennis career.

My story would not be possible without Gloria, my wife since 1964. We married when I was twenty-two and Gloria was twenty. We met in August 1960, when I was eighteen, and Gloria was sixteen. She was soon to be a senior at White Station High School, the newest public high school in the most eastern part of the city. She was my first love and only love, and I was hers. Gloria spent two years at Sophie Newcomb College (now Tulane) in New Orleans but returned to Memphis to be with me and finish her degree at Southwestern, now Rhodes College. She graduated Phi Beta Kappa. During our almost sixty years together, Gloria has been a mom, a housewife, a tutor to our children and many teenagers in preparation for the college entrance exams, a bookkeeper for the family, and a Shakespeare reader. As the role of women has changed during our life together, Gloria has changed with the times. I often say I have been married to six different wives.

Gloria was the daughter of two German Jewish refugees. Her mother was related to Sam Shainberg, a wealthy merchant family in Memphis. In 1938, Sam Shainberg sponsored her mom and her uncle to get them out of Germany and away from Hitler. They came to Memphis to work for his company. Gloria's mom was nineteen and her uncle was eighteen when they arrived in the United States. Both of them went to work for the Shainbergs' company, and then her uncle was drafted into the U.S. Army. Like many of the male German Jewish immigrants drafted, Gloria's uncle was sent to the Pacific arena for security reasons rather than back to Germany. Gloria's grandparents on her mother's side were not able to get out of Germany. German soldiers shot and killed them and thousands of others in a field in Latvia in 1941.

Gloria's father had miraculously escaped from Berlin in 1937 and was able to get to the United States, where he was sponsored by his sister who had come to the U.S. earlier with her husband, who had dual citizenship. Upon reaching New York, her father learned that a Jewish merchant in Memphis, Leo Levy, would hire a Jewish refugee from Nazi Germany, and he immediately got on a train and came to Memphis to work for him at Levy's Department Store.

Gloria's father and mother met at a party for newcomers in 1942. She was sixteen years younger than he. Determined to become Americanized, Gloria's father had changed his name from Cohen to Cornell. So, it was Eric Cornell who married Helga Robins in 1942. The name Robins had been changed from Rabinowitsch. Gloria's mother never wanted her German experiences mentioned in her house while Gloria was growing up. There was too much pain.

Grateful to be American citizens, Gloria's parents proudly flew the flag in front of their homes. Their escapes paved the way for the lives of their children, grandchildren, and great-grandchildren. In 2001, our first grandson was born. We now have nine wonderful grandchildren, five girls and four boys. My three sons all have wonderful wives.

As I embark on my eighties, I am having another dream. And it makes me conclude that possibly we do not actually change that much during the span of our lives. When I went out into my big backyard garden this morning to gather some tomatoes, okra, and eggplant, and to pick some figs, I found myself having this thought: Perhaps, with some luck, I will continue to work until I am ninety. By then, eight of my grandchildren will all be over the age of twenty-one and old enough to go to work. Maybe one of them will decide to come to Memphis and move into our house with the big backyard. Gloria and I can move into a nursing home. And then they can take over Felsenthal Financial Services.

But even if that doesn't happen, my life will still amount to a dream come true.

Gloria and Eddie Felsenthal, 2019   Eddie Felsenthal, White River in Colorado, 2018

13 - Churchill Roberts

2007 - Uncovering Untold Twentieth-Century Stories

In 2003, I was a professor of journalism teaching documentary filmmaking at the University of Florida in Gainesville when my colleagues and I began work on a film about an American soldier during World War II. His name was Vernon Tott. While traveling across Germany as the war was ending in April of 1945, he and his infantry division happened upon the liberation of a Nazi concentration camp's forced labor unit in a place called Ahlem. Tott was so shocked at the starving, emaciated, enslaved people he saw that he pulled out a pocket camera he carried with him and took photos. He even took some photos of the dead bodies of prisoners who hadn't survived the brutal work conditions at Ahlem. When Tott returned to the United States, he had the photos developed. But he didn't do anything else with them, except put them in a shoebox and move on with his life. Fifty years later, a survivor of that labor camp, who was one of the people in the pictures, found Tott and asked to see the photos. Revisiting those old images sent Vernon Tott on a quest to find other Holocaust survivors who appeared in the nineteen photos he took on that day of liberation. Our film, *Angel of Ahlem*, documented Tott's search.

In 2007, *Angel of Ahlem* was screened at Lincoln Center in New York. Of course, it was a thrill to get such exposure for our work. But the part of the night I remember the most was when Henry Kissinger, the first Jewish U.S. Secretary of State and a Nobel Peace Prize winner, got up to introduce the film. Kissinger had been in the same infantry outfit as Vernon Tott. So, he had witnessed the same scene at Ahlem that day in 1945. Kissinger's introduction was moving. But then, he stopped midway through his formal remarks and looked across the audience. Kissinger asked if there were any survivors of Ahlem in the room, and if so, would they come on stage and have a photo made with him. As cameras flashed and tears flowed, about a dozen men proudly made their way to the stage and surrounded Kissinger. It was a magical, full circle moment -- one I think everyone in that room always remembered.

When I started work on *Angel of Ahlem*, I had no idea I would be devoting almost ten years of my life to producing two films about the Holocaust -- that one, and another called *The Last Flight of Petr Ginz*, about a young Jewish boy from Prague who was an artist and wrote books and magazine articles. He was sent to a concentration camp at age fourteen and continued to create. But he was killed at Auschwitz when he was sixteen. Much of his work survived and was found years later. Our film showed the story of Petr and the tragedy of his death, through his writing and art.

Although I went to a high school in Memphis with a number of Jewish students, I never had even one conversation with any of them about the Holocaust, or for that matter, about the civil rights movement which was unfolding in front of our eyes in the late 1950s. But a decade later, higher education, and particularly documentary film, began to open up a new world for me. It was a world light-years away from my Memphis roots.

Like many white kids in my hometown of Memphis, I had what I remember as an idyllic childhood. I was an only child, shielded from the deep poverty in our city, though my family was far from rich. And I was shielded from the racial injustice Black Memphians lived with every day, though I later realized it was all around me, once I learned to see it, just beneath the surface. While Memphis in the 1940s and 1950s was about as "Deep South" and segregated as one could imagine, I don't recall thinking of it that way at the time. What was instilled in me was a romanticized version, a *Gone with the Wind*-like picture of Memphis, the cotton capital of the world, home to sons and daughters of the Confederacy, with no mention of its also being home to the sons and daughters of enslaved people.

My grandfather was a cotton broker. He bought, sold, and classified cotton and had an office on Front Street, the first street on the bluff above the Mississippi River where Memphis was built. That stretch of Front Street was often called Cotton Row for the many cotton offices that lined it. Some of my earliest recollections are of my grandfather taking me with him on trips to inspect cotton fields. While my grandfather, whom I called Pop, met with farmers and businessmen and told them what they might expect for their cotton crop, I would sit patiently in the car, knowing that afterward I would be treated to a milk shake or banana split. My grandfather is buried in Elmwood Cemetery, one of the oldest cemeteries in Memphis, and the resting place of twenty Confederate generals and dotted with monuments to many more Confederate soldiers.

I did get a glimpse of somewhere far from all that when I was six, and my mother and I joined my father in Paris, France. After being discharged from the Army, he had taken a civilian job with the American Graves Registration Command (AGRC) in Europe, whose mission was to identify American casualties, find their next of kin, and determine whether a deceased soldier should be disinterred and reburied in the United States or moved to an American cemetery in Europe. That first month in Paris I lived in the Hotel Wagram on the Rue de Rivoli, across the street from the Tuileries Garden and the world-famous Louvre Museum. From my hotel window, I could see the giant Ferris wheel and merry-go-round and ankle-deep pond where I sailed a little boat my parents bought me. I attended the

American School of Paris and had to walk a few blocks to the American Embassy to catch the bus.

After a few months, my father decided we should move to Versailles, to be closer to AGRC headquarters in the Trianon Palace Hotel next to the famous Palace of Versailles. The Trianon had hosted many famous guests since its opening in 1910. It was there in 1919 that French Prime Minister Georges Clemenceau dictated the terms of the Treaty of Versailles which brought about a formal ending to World War I. My family and I shared a large two-story home with another AGRC family, and I switched from the American School in Paris to a small, private French school. I have no recollection of learning French. But I spoke it, because everyone in the school spoke it.

Despite the aftermath of war conditions throughout Europe, my parents took me skiing in St. Moritz and Garmisch-Partenkirchen, and they made sure travel and sightseeing were as important in my life as school. I still have photos of some of the train rides, sitting in a compartment looking out the window, not knowing what to make of the rubble in the background. I wish I could say I asked questions about the war or about the plight of the six million Jews who perished. But I didn't. I was six years old. The Tuileries Garden and Palace of Versailles were my playgrounds, and my only responsibility was to accompany my mother when she went shopping. I was her interpreter.

After a year, my father decided to return to Memphis. AGRC funding was uncertain, subject to the whims of Congress, and I suspect my father was homesick. I have all the letters he wrote from Europe during and after the war and those my mother wrote from France. They weren't intellectual letters about the horrors of war or the human condition. They were quite practical: "Please send money; there's not a new bicycle to be found in Paris." My mother was lamenting the fact that she couldn't fulfill my Christmas wish list. "Please tell Alfred to send more cigarettes." It turns out my cousin's father Alfred was a tobacco distributor. The French franc was practically worthless, American dollars hard to come by, but cigarettes -- they were like gold. You could buy everything with cigarettes. And my father did. I think the "everybody does it" excuse was his rationale. Thank goodness I was a child and unaware of the black market.

Back in Memphis, my French practically vanished. "Bonjour. Comment allez-vous aujourd'hui?" had morphed into "How y'all doin' today?" My father returned to work in the cotton business, but by the early 1950s he had left that industry and was working for American Airlines. The benefits were terrific. Employees accumulated mileage according to their years of service and had unlimited mileage when they were on vacation. That meant my father, mother, and I could fly for free wherever American Airlines went, in the United States or abroad. Our first trip was to Mexico, where I developed a strong distaste for bullfighting or any form of animal cruelty. That same year one of my beloved uncles gave me a BB gun, and after killing a bird, I retrieved it, looked at its beautiful yellow feathers, blood-stained, then buried it. I put away the BB gun and lost any interest in killing for sport.

During the summer of 1955, my father allowed me to travel by myself to Los Angeles to visit my bedridden great-grandmother. But I did much more than that. I visited cities in the Southwest and jumped back on a plane every time I needed a meal or a place to sleep. When I returned to Memphis, I asked an agent at the ticket counter where my dad was. The agent said he was in New York on business. So, I hopped on the plane again and headed for New York, where I found him at the American Airlines office. We then went to a Yankees baseball game before heading home. The American Airlines agents based in Memphis thought my summer trips sounded hilarious and encouraged me to write about them and enter a contest sponsored by Sabena, a Belgian airline. The challenge was to write about a unique experience related to air travel. My story won. The reward was an all-expenses-paid trip to Europe for two. I gave the prize to my parents. They went in 1956 and had a wonderful time for the first week, visiting places they had lived and seeing Rome for the first time. But during the second week, my mother was in so much pain the trip had to be cut short.

In the mid-1950s my mother was diagnosed with breast cancer. She had a mastectomy and thought the disease was behind her. But in 1955, she began experiencing pain in her hip and then throughout her body. The cancer had returned with a vengeance. She went to Houston's MD Anderson Clinic, one of the top cancer treatment centers in the world. The doctors there did everything they could to save her, but it was too late. The cancer had entered her lymph nodes and spread to other organs.

In the fall of 1956, I entered Central High School. My mother died the next summer of 1957 just before I entered the eleventh grade. For a while, my father tried to put on a brave face. But grief and alcohol began to take their toll on him. High school should have been the best years of my life up to that point, but family problems, immaturity, and self-pity overwhelmed me and caused me to flounder throughout my high school years -- and well into college. Just before my senior year, my father decided to sell our home, and we moved in with my grandmother. Shortly after I started my senior year, my dad announced he needed a fresh start and was moving to California -- by himself.

By then, I had gotten a job as a soda jerk and delivery boy at Kessler's Pharmacy on Madison Avenue. I was not cut out to be a soda jerk. On one of my first days, a group of girls from a nearby Catholic high school came by for ice cream. I lifted the cooler top, but a fog of vapor from the dry ice made it impossible to see the different flavors. I solved the problem by taking a deep breath and blowing across all the open bins of ice cream. I thought the poor pharmacist would have a heart attack. He quickly handed me a prescription to deliver and turned over the fountain to a more experienced soda jerk.

Before he left for California, my father dropped by Kessler's Pharmacy to say goodbye. He had purchased an MG sports car and had it loaded to capacity. I walked out to the parking lot and shook hands with him and watched him drive up Madison Avenue on his way out of town on the Memphis & Arkansas Bridge. That evening as I walked home, I felt the whole world had come crashing down on me. In the short space of two years, I had lost my mother, and for all practical purposes, my father. And I was only sixteen.

But I was looking at the half-empty glass. I had two wonderful and wonderfully strong grandmothers and many close and supportive friends. Soon, I had graduated from Central and was attending the University of Tennessee in Knoxville. I didn't take academics too seriously. My grades were anything but spectacular. The best thing about my time at UT was that I met a Knoxville girl my senior year -- Gay Wilson. We took an audiology class together. She was at the top of the class. I was at the other end. But we hit it off. We were engaged shortly after we graduated, and we married at the end of 1963.

I wasn't sure what I wanted to do with my life, but because of Gay, and, later, our two children, the glass began to appear half-full again. I worked for a time in the home offices of Dobbs House in Memphis, which had restaurants, snack bars, and airline catering services throughout the United States. A high-powered chef from New Jersey was brought in to test recipes for a prototype restaurant. I was assigned as his assistant. That was when I learned how to cook. The first thing the chef demanded was that I quit smoking. "You can't taste food if you smoke," he said. I never smoked again. To this day, I love trying new recipes and fixing my favorite ones -- especially dishes from Italy and France -- fried zucchini blossoms, coq au vin, tagliatelle alla Bolognese, grouper avec lemon beurre blanc. In a million years, I could never have seen myself taking a home economics course in high school. Boys didn't do that. And yet as a young adult, cooking became a passion and has turned into a lifelong hobby.

I enjoyed consuming food but not working in the food business. My wife and I decided, therefore, to broaden our horizons. One year, as

Christmas gifts we gave each other a course at Memphis State University (now the University of Memphis). I took a class in Broadcasting and Film, while she took a class in Speech Pathology. Those courses changed our lives. Pretty soon, all I could think about was being in the education field. Thanks to former Central High School coach Malcolm Phillips, who by the late 1960s had moved into a position with the Memphis school board, I landed a job as an instructor of communication in a program funded by the U.S. government's Manpower Development Training Act. The day I first walked into that classroom I was sure of what I wanted to do with my life. I wanted to be an educator.

My major professor at Memphis State was David Yellin, a former radio, tv, and theater producer in New York City who had moved to the South in the mid-1960s to teach broadcasting and film. One day in 1968 he told me, "If you decide on a career as a university professor, you have to get a PhD. Otherwise, you'll always be treated as a second-class citizen." I got the message. That year, Martin Luther King, Jr. was assassinated in Memphis. Shortly afterward, David Yellin and his wife Carol Lynn, an editor and journalist at *Reader's Digest*, founded the Memphis Search for Meaning Committee and produced an oral history of the sanitation workers' strike which King had come to Memphis to support. My role in that project was to go around to all the local Memphis television stations and gather television news footage, including the outtakes, of the strike and the aftermath of the assassination. That footage became part of the extensive archive of the strike produced by the project. It is all now housed at the University of Memphis library. Some of the footage I gathered for the archive would later become the basis for my first film, *Keep Your Trash*.

At Memphis State, I enjoyed not only filmmaking but also research -- especially quantitative research. My thesis was a quantitative study of African American students' attitudes toward television. I enjoyed quantitative research so much that when applying for my doctoral studies, I picked the most quantitatively oriented communications program in the country -- the University of Iowa. There, I studied under a famous communication professor, Samuel L. Becker. He was a scholar's scholar, one of the most erudite, insightful, and prolific academicians I've ever met. He was also the department chair. So, the year I was writing my dissertation, I persuaded him to give me the funds to make the film about the Memphis sanitation strike and assassination of Martin Luther King, Jr.

While I was enjoying the exciting and high-pressured life of a doctoral student, my wife, Gay, managed the household, which included two children. She also commuted to Cedar Rapids five days a week to work as a speech therapist in the public schools. A few years later, when we moved to Florida, she became the director of a speech and hearing clinic -- and continued to manage the kids and the household.

I completed *Keep Your Trash* and screened it at the University of Iowa at about the same time I defended my dissertation. My colleagues were very complimentary, but we all wondered what people in Memphis would think of it. I was anxious to find out, so I contacted the station manager at WMCT, Mori Greiner. I had interned at WMCT, the NBC affiliate in Memphis, and knew Mr. Greiner was a progressive manager. He invited me to Memphis and arranged for a private screening with a few Memphis insiders at the station. After the screening, the eight to ten people in the room stood and slowly walked out. They didn't utter a single word. Greiner came over to me and whispered something to the effect of "very powerful film," followed by a pause. Then he said, "Of course, you understand we can't show a film like that in Memphis." I was disappointed. But Memphis was still too polarized, too traumatized to deal with a film that struck at its racist core. Years later the local PBS station in Memphis, WKNO, did air the film, and no one protested.

Until the assassination of Martin Luther King, Jr., I had been, at best, a bystander in the civil rights movement. Many historians cite the years 1954 to 1968 as the key time period of the movement. I became aware in 1968, at the tail end of that period. My parents and grandparents were from the South and had accepted segregation as both moral and just. They were not early adopters of ideas about desegregation. Nor was I. It took the assassination of a major civil rights figure to make me rethink my inherited notions about race and social justice. I am not sure my parents ever changed their views. But as part of my doctoral studies, I took a course on race relations which helped me understand the long legacy of racial inequity that the Memphis sanitation strike had been all about.

Some of my early quantitative research dealt with the stereotypical portrayals of Black people or the absence of Black people in television entertainment and news programming. Later in my career, my major achievements were two documentary films about remarkable Black activists that aired nationally on PBS -- *Freedom Never Dies: The Legacy of Harry T. Moore* (2001) and *Negroes with Guns: Rob Williams and Black Power* (2006).

My three colleagues and I began working on those civil rights films while also administering The Documentary Institute, a graduate program in documentary filmmaking in the College of Journalism and Communications at the University of Florida. With the aid of eminent historians such as Sam Proctor, David Chalmers, and David Colburn, we crafted stories about little-known or unsung heroes of the civil rights movement. Both the Harry T. Moore and Rob Williams films would later be winners of the Organization of American Historians' Erik Barnouw Award for best historical documentary. At the time, only two other filmmakers had received the OAH award twice -- Ken Burns, the director of numerous iconic PBS documentaries, and Henry Hampton, who produced the definitive twentieth-century documentary about civil rights called *Eyes on the Prize.*

Another film-related experience that stands out in my forty-plus years of teaching and making documentaries was when I arranged to interview the filmmaker Leni Riefenstahl. She had introduced Adolph Hitler to the people of Germany and to the rest of the world with her 1934 blockbuster pro-Nazi film, *Triumph of the Will,* the most notorious propaganda film of all time. After WWII, most of the worldwide film industry shunned Riefenstahl. In the 1970s, Francis Ford Coppola, director of *The Godfather* trilogy, invited Riefenstahl to a film festival in Telluride, Colorado, to screen her 1932 feature film, *The Blue Light*. She had been both its star and its director. At Telluride, she was greeted with protests as well as applause.

As a film scholar, I was interested in Riefenstahl's life, particularly her documentary work, and thanks to an academic connection, I was able to contact her. I wrote and said I'd be interested in interviewing her if the opportunity ever arose. Several months later, and much to my surprise, I received a note from her secretary saying Riefenstahl would be diving in the Bahamas -- an activity she took up in her seventies -- and before returning to Germany, would have an overnight layover in Ft. Lauderdale. If I wanted an interview, I would have to be at her hotel on the morning she arrived. I later learned that the day before my interview, she had met with Dan Rather for a television interview that aired on *60 Minutes*.

To most of the Western press and to the public, Leni Riefenstahl was the personification of evil -- a woman who used her art to prop up one of the worst monsters history has ever known. I was so worried that my interview might be seen as a form of acceptance or admiration, I called my University of Iowa adviser, Sam Becker, who was Jewish, and asked him what I should do. I was particularly interested in the opinion of his wife, Ruth, who had been in a concentration camp and had escaped Nazi Germany thanks to the English rescue mission called the Kindertransport. Ruth and Sam didn't hesitate -- I should keep the appointment. I was, after all, a scholar, not a fan.

I recorded the interview, and afterward, as a polite gesture, Riefenstahl said if I were ever in Germany, perhaps we could continue the conversation. I liked that idea because I felt I had just scratched the surface in learning about her life. Several years later, before traveling to Florence, Italy to teach for the fall semester, I decided to contact Riefenstahl to see if she really was serious about a follow-up interview. Months later, I received a telegram from Riefenstahl inviting me to meet her at her home just southwest of Munich on Lake Starnberg. Walking into her home was an eerie feeling, like entering the belly of the beast. Riefenstahl explained she would have only an hour or so. As it turned out, she spent almost the entire day with me. During one interval when she was out of the room, I glanced around and spotted a book on her coffee table -- *Hitler's Weltanschauung* (Hitler's Worldview). I felt revulsion. But I believed getting her point of view on film, as much as I disagreed with her choice to make such propaganda films, was an important part of my work as a scholar.

When my colleagues and I began producing documentaries on a regular basis in the 1980s, we did some work in Latin America. After producing a film on Panama, our first to be aired nationally on PBS, we turned our attention to Nicaragua and then to Cuba. We couldn't get into Cuba as journalists, so we tagged along with an academic group and filmed when we could. The short documentary we produced was about the role of religion in Cuba. Later, I was invited by the now defunct United States Information Agency (USIA) to conduct the Congressionally mandated evaluation of Radio Marti, the U.S. radio service to Cuba -- a gift to the Cuban American community in Miami for its support of Ronald Reagan in the presidential campaigns of 1980 and 1984. Skeptics in Congress demanded an outside evaluation of the service for the first three years of its operation. For two of those years, I was selected as the outside evaluator. On the whole, I gave the operation high marks, although I noted that a complementary service, TV Marti, was a waste of money.

After conducting the evaluations, I suggested to my colleagues that we try to obtain press passes to Cuba and make a film about U.S.-Cuba relations. I pitched the idea to Cuba's Foreign Ministry and accepted an invitation to travel to Cuba to discuss it. On my initial visit, I indicated that in addition to talking to government officials, we wanted to speak to dissidents, because failing to do so would suggest the Cuban government orchestrated the trip. I mentioned several prominent dissidents. A representative from the Foreign Ministry, later to be our handler in Cuba, said he had no objection.

Several months later I arrived with a film crew. We learned that a group of well-known Cuban artists and writers had just signed a Declaration for Democracy -- demanding more personal freedom for Cubans. One of the dissidents offered me an interview with the signers. I jumped at the chance. In order to avoid government scrutiny, we used two film crews, one which would serve as a decoy while the other slipped away unnoticed and headed for a secret rendezvous. We interviewed several prominent artists -- a poet and a number of painters -- who took great risks in talking to us.

On our final day in Cuba, just as were celebrating the explosive inter-views we had gotten, our handler in the Ministry of Foreign Relations called me. He was most upset and said the Attorney General of Cuba, Ramón de la Cruz Ochoa, wanted to see me immediately. Whatever cordial relations existed with Cuban officials evaporated in the Attorney General's presence. He accused my colleagues and me of causing several dissidents to violate the terms of their "conditional liberty" by engaging in subversive political behavior. He said furthermore I had misled Cuban authorities about the true purpose of our film. My colleagues and I were then ordered to remain in our hotel until further notice. While we awaited our fate, the Ministry of Interior posted security guards at all hotel entrances. A few hours later, our handler from the Ministry of Foreign Relations called to say I needed to hand over everything we had recorded in Cuba. Doing so would no doubt have resulted in prison sentences for the artists, one of whom was the famous poet Maria Elena Cruz Varela. So, I politely declined. The han-dler was so upset with my obstinance he could barely speak to me.

Hours passed. Another call. The Foreign Ministry official informed me that police would be raiding our rooms. I told him that was unneces-sary. We would put all the tapes on a table -- and then added this caveat: "You do understand that if you seize the tapes, we'll hold a press conference if and when we return to Miami, and tell everyone what happened to us." I had just played my only ace.

In 1988, Cuba agreed to participate in the Pan American Games in Indianapolis on the condition that the United States would participate when the games were held in Cuba four years later. Fidel Castro knew that hosting the games would be a propaganda coup, and he committed millions of scarce dollars to building venues. One spark, however, would be all it would take to make the U.S. reconsider participating. I was banking on the fact that since it was now 1992, and not long after our visit the games were set for Cuba, our press conference would be the spark.

Several hours passed. No police raid. Finally, I got a call from the handler. We could keep the tapes -- as long as we allowed Cuban authorities to view them in our room. Pause. I again declined. The handler hung up the phone. By this time, we had been negotiating nonstop for almost twenty-four hours. After what seemed an eternity, the phone rang again. In a curt voice, the handler said, "Pack your bags and be in the lobby in thirty minutes." We did as we were told, not knowing whether we were headed to prison or to the airport. Fortunately, it was the latter. We were placed on a charter flight and thirty-five minutes later landed in Miami. We had our tapes, so there was no need for a press conference. The next year, *Campaign for Cuba* aired nationally on PBS.

Fifteen years after that, in 2008, my colleagues and I were at the pinnacle of our careers. Our many films had garnered much national attention. *The Independent*, a film trade publication, had named our graduate program in documentary film, The Documentary Institute, one of the ten best in North America -- along with Duke, Stanford, and NYU. It seemed things couldn't get much better, but they could get much worse -- and they did. The recession of 2008 took its toll on higher education. Florida was particularly hard hit. Administrators were faced with one cutback after another. Unfortunately, my college had a new dean who decided to cut our entire budget in 2010. In one swing of the axe, he eliminated a program that had taken years to build. Despite a student-led petition and letters from colleagues around the country, the dean stood his ground, and the president and provost deferred to the dean. No sooner had word spread that the documentary program was being cut than my colleagues and I began receiving calls from other universities.

I was in Israel working on the Petr Ginz film. When I got home, Wake Forest University had an attractive offer on the table. One of us would move there right away, the rest to follow the next year. There was just one problem. We had recently received a sizeable grant to produce the Petr Ginz film, but the funding, from a Florida foundation, wasn't transportable. In the end, I stayed at University of Florida, and my colleagues went to Wake Forest and transferred the documentary program there.

Although I traveled to Winston-Salem about every other year after 2010 to visit my former colleagues and work with Wake's documentary students, I was somewhat at loose ends. Then, in the mid-2010s, as happened so many times in my life, I was spurred to embark on a new adventure.

For a number of years my graduate students from the People's Republic of China would ask me why I hadn't traveled to China. I had been to so many places -- but not China. Finally, their urging prompted me to take a vacation there with my wife. I was able to reconnect with some of those former students and to lecture at China's most prestigious film school, the Beijing Film Academy. Those students then challenged me to make a documentary in China. And so, at the tender age of seventy-one, I began traveling to China on a regular basis -- eight trips during the next nine years. For five of those years, I worked on *The Curse of the Terracotta Warriors*, a film about a group of peasant farmers who discovered one of the great archaeological treasures of the world -- the Terracotta Warriors, guardians of the tomb of China's first emperor. Filming in China is difficult under any circumstances. Censorship, including self-censorship by people I interviewed, is ingrained in the Chinese psyche. Partly to lessen that, I decided to use an all-Chinese production crew and to produce the film in

Mandarin Chinese as well as in English. I have continued to work on making documentaries in China, even in my eighties.

Through the last two decades, I have continually postponed thinking about retirement by doing the work I love. Also, I don't have any real hobbies besides cooking. But I don't need to retire to do that. I've always loved sports, but to say I was even an average athlete would be a stretch. My wife took up running and won so many races she filled a bookcase with trophies. From time to time she reminds me that I have the dubious distinction of being the only member of the family not to run the Boston Marathon. I didn't run a fast enough qualifying time. There's a reason that when I was growing up my nickname was Turtle. So, I keep on making films and teaching at the university, enjoying my time with the students and my colleagues.

Another enjoyment is watching the growth of our children and grandchildren. My daughter, Kathy, became an award-winning high school science teacher, and my son, Churchill IV (Church), became an environmental engineer and eventually opened his own business. My two grandchildren, both boys, excel in academics and athletics. They are gazelles on the track team, a far cry from their grandfather, Turtle.

I've often thought about how serendipitous my life has been. There was never any real plan. In junior high, I said I wanted to be a plastic surgeon. In high school, I considered going to college at the Missouri School of Mines. I have never been one to reflect much on where I was in life and where I was headed. I just more or less gravitated toward things I enjoyed and could do well. I often tell students how lucky I am.

The filmmaker who coined the term documentary, a Scotsman by the name of John Grierson, once said the first principle of documentary is that it's about today, not about yesterday, and the only good film is the one you're going to make tomorrow. I take Grierson's optimism about filmmaking as a challenge to keep going, not to rest on one's laurels, but to find new and better ways to make films. That recipe applies to more than filmmaking. It also applies to life—seeing each day as a new chance to learn, and even at this late stage for me, to improve.

Churchill and Gay Roberts   Churchill Roberts and film crew
Angel of Ahlem screening   *The Last Flight of Peter Ginz*
Iowa, 2007   Czech Republic, 2008

14 - Jimmy Biles

2022 - Nine Lives in Nine Decades

I am in my early eighties and should have died by now. Somehow, though, I seem to have been given nine lives. As a baby, I was covered with red stinging ants while lying on a blanket outside a tin shack in the Louisiana bayou country. At three, I fell into the current of the Mississippi River, but luckily and quickly I was fished out. At five, I had a severe allergic reaction to a bee sting. I had polio at age six, and at ten caught Black Water Fever, causing me to turn yellow at camp. When I was twelve, Sardis Lake nearly claimed me on a very cold spring day because my Penguin sailboat capsized in a heavy gust of wind. At twenty, the cypress trees of the Great Dismal Swamp nearly downed our Cessna airplane while trying to find a safe landing when low on gas in zero-zero conditions. At thirty-seven, a deranged patient shot me in my head, and I escaped a second bullet by playing dead. I think I have challenged God's omnipotence and help a bit too much. But with fair certainty, my nine lives are coming to a close now.

Because as I start my ninth decade on earth, I have been diagnosed with metastatic cancer.

It's quite an experience to get this diagnosis after my long career as a cancer surgeon. I have held the hands of dying patients -- sensing their fears of death, their grief, and for some, the agony of dying. Now I am in their shoes and struggling with the same emotions and pain. Am I holding my own hand the best way? What creates calm and comfort? Have I prepared myself? Have I asked for forgiveness where I should have? Have I said goodbye to friends and family? Does my spirituality support me? Have I passed on the proper legacies? Do I have the courage to manage my pain? Do I have the trust in the help I need? Can I have some control of my death? Do I need a "Death with Dignity" agreement?

Even though I learned all this stuff in medical school and in my practice, I am still turning up with questions on how to approach my own death.

I think of my legacy, and of my lifelong love of medicine. And I realize now that my father's legacy set up my own. I remember the many afternoon and weekend trips with my father to our nearby Memphis Baptist Hospital, tagging along on his patient rounds. This started when I was a young boy in the 1940s and went on through my teenage years in the 1950s. I got to go into patients' rooms and chat with them. I saw my father change the dressings. I flirted at the nurses' stations as my father wrote his orders. I kibitzed with many doctors in the doctor's lounge. And my reward was a chocolate malted milkshake in the hospital drug store, a treat I have loved ever since.

On many weekends, we would travel from Memphis to Sumner, Mississippi -- our family seat, where my grandfather and uncle practiced general medicine. Sumner was totally segregated then, and it would later be the site of the Emmett Till murder trial. My father made country rounds down dusty roads among the farmhouses, the tin shacks, and the poor nursing homes, treating both Black and white patients without regard to pay, applying his surgical and medical skills. As usual, he took me along, and I saw a vast assortment of maladies. Father would discuss the how and the why of each medical problem with me, and its treatment. I once saw a boil the size of a watermelon. And I will never forget his challenge to the unknown -- an inspiration for me. There were no antibiotics in those days and people often died of infections. Remedies like herbs weren't commonly prescribed. But he figured out that using the herb foxglove, for instance, to prevent heart failure with otherwise untreatable pneumonia, would give the body a fighting chance. And it worked in many cases.

At age five, I had my tonsils removed in the small operating room at the Sumner clinic to prevent strep throat. My father did the surgery and was assisted by my uncle and grandfather. I remember their kindness as they held the mask to my face and gave me the ether. I awoke with quite a sore throat and was treated to ice cream from the parents churning it outside. As I got older, I was allowed to assist with the ether, and with aspirating patients to keep the surgical field visibly clear.

I caught polio around age six and stayed a goodly length of time in the hospital. My mother brought in mounds of comic books to pass the days. I don't remember much pain except for the spinal taps, but I escaped the misery of those lying endlessly in the iron lungs down the hall. Those sights never escaped me. It was my first real taste of being a patient, and of being quite helpless. Another sickness that showed me what a doctor could do to relieve a patient's suffering was that time I was stung by a bee. I suddenly swelled up all over and could barely breath. The itching was beyond belief. Dad happened to be there, gave me some medicine, and dumped me into a bathtub with a very cold oatmeal brew. Mercifully, I got better fairly quickly as my very worried father hovered over me.

Even the hunting and fishing I did down on the farm turned out to prepare me for becoming a doctor. I learned a lot of anatomy from cleaning game animals and fish, and I learned not to be squeamish, especially as my father or uncle pointed out the various organs and inner workings of the animals. Most of all, though, I aspired to the care, courtesy, and under-standing my father gave his patients, the respect he got, and the love he had for what he did. I liked people. I loved problem solving. I loved a challenge. I was good with my hands. And I admired the integrity of the medical pro-fession -- you don't argue with Mother Nature. It didn't hurt that I would also be one of five doctors in the family -- along with my grandfather, my uncle, my father, and now my son.

One of the major contributors to my life was growing up in a relatively sophisticated city but having access to the country life of the Mississippi Delta too. During the 1940s war years, we grew our own vegetables, raised goats, cows, and pigs for milk and meat, churned our own butter, and made soap over an open fire in a large kettle. All the farm kids, Black and white, played together. We made a chariot together to be pulled by our old mule. I picked some cotton and even with assistance got to plow behind a mule. Later, there were tractors, jeeps, and hunting and fishing that the city kids never got to experience. I rambled through the blacksmith forge, the mechanic's shop, the cypress swamps and woods, handling many of the animals with their breeding, branding, and veterinary care. This was seeing Mother Nature -- beautiful, but down and dirty too.

Becoming a doctor requires a broad and lengthy education. And it started in earnest for me at Central High School. At that time, women were allowed few careers other than motherhood, but teaching was one of them. And my teachers were the best and the brightest. Ms. Mauzy's math classes taught me to focus, think, and analyze. Ms. Clinton, my English teacher, was always available in her loving way. She helped put conceptional think-ing into understandable expression. The biology, chemistry, and physics courses of Ms. Green taught me a fascination and curiosity about life and enriched my spirituality.

In high school I also learned what friendship is all about -- bonding with peers and learning to make our bonds strong. Athletics and dances were where those friendships formed and played out. In football there was something special about slugging through the mud, heat, cold, and very smelly locker rooms with both teammates and guys you were competing against, all focused on a singular, communal purpose. And it was very special to dance your heart out with girlfriends, especially since we were there for the birth of Rock and Roll in Memphis.

During those early years, I also acquired a lifelong passion for sailing. At eighty, I still cruise and race. But I first found sailing while reading *National Geographic* magazines as a kid. I mowed yards to pay for a small sailboat and have been enraptured ever since. How does one describe the inner sensations of driving your own boat through waves, powered by your understanding of the wind? Trial and error taught me, along with many books. Sailing forced me to study elementary aerodynamics and hydrodynamics. And it taught me how a passion feels. I later felt a similar passion for medicine, as well as for my family.

I suffered culture shock when I went off to college. Yale University was an all-boys institution at the time. The "up East" food didn't compare to Southern cooking. There was no decent music. The cold was pervasive. A tie had to be worn at every meal, and competing with the Eastern private school educations was major league for a minor leaguer. It took a while, but eventually I made a lot of good friends, gained parity in academics, learned to play squash, and was quite successful on the Yale sailing team. I majored in American Studies. It was one of the better choices in my life. As I knew I was going to graduate school for medicine, I did not have to use college for a vocational education. I was lucky in so many ways.

Acceptance at Columbia University, College of Physicians and Surgeons for graduate school cemented my career course. Columbia was great all the way through -- great friends and great professors -- a wonderful hands-on experience. We were taught not to think categorically or formulaically, but rather physiologically and pathologically, understanding all the variable pieces of the puzzle at hand. Know what you know, and know what you don't and can't know -- no assumptions, ask or find out.

My great research experience there provided me an approach to problem solving that has endured.

During the last year of medical school, I knew I wanted to do surgery, and I thought Urology was what I wanted. Urologists treated all age groups and genders, from birth defects to old-age failings, and cancer. Both medicine and surgery knowledge and skills would be used. For my internship, I wanted a good experience, preferably on a coast for sailing. I got my first choice, a general surgical position on the Tulane Division of Charity Hospital in New Orleans.

It was the toughest year of my life, but also probably the best single medical year of my life. I had been to New Orleans before and loved the French Quarter and its music, the ambiance of its architecture and weather, the Southern Hospitality and its food. I had cousins there who could, on those rare occasions I was free, spend time with me. They had roots into the swamps for hunting and fishing and knew every out-of-the-way tavern with the best food in Louisiana. And one cousin-in-law had a Dragon sailboat for me to use on Lake Pontchartrain. All these personal delights were only tasted in between the rigors of days and nights of seemingly nonstop work.

Charity Hospital had several-hundred residents and interns. I was lucky to have been one of only eight to get a straight surgical internship, which meant I rotated through many services -- general surgery, cardiac, ortho, urology, ER, internal medicine, and neurology. Little did I realize the intensity of the work. I would work in the hospital for three straight days and two nights before having one night off. I learned to sleep during short interludes, although always stalked by sleep deprivation. It is difficult to say this, but I did sleep standing up, frozen still, at the operating table a few times, holding retractors to keep the wound open for the surgeon. In medicine Mother Nature never lets go, whether it's you or the patient. Which is one of the beauties of medicine. It demands the truth in confronting disease, comforting patients, and relating to fellow doctors.

The volume of work at Charity Hospital was endless, from the operating room that was constantly running, to the packed clinics and clinic procedures, the frequent ER calls, consults on other services such as medicine or orthopedics, ICU patient management, and care of patients on the wards who needed frequent attendance. We interns had to do a lot, as hands were needed to get all the work done.

Then, I went on to a residency position in Urology at Johns Hopkins. It was an entirely different, top-down, "yes sir", authoritarian environment -- very didactic and academically oriented. The real effort for all of us young doctors was to learn how to be a complete surgeon. We saw an almost endless array of cases that other physicians or hospitals deemed too difficult to handle, or that needed specialized care, experimental care, or newer treatments. We learned surgery and just about all of urology.

To make up for the low pay along the way, and personal needs, I moonlighted. At Columbia, I ran the Blood Bank on weekends. At Johns Hopkins, I worked at Planned Parenthood. I also performed about eight vasectomies on an occasional Saturday morning, making about $25 a case. Other weekends I was an ER doctor, facing all the maladies of life -- very good additional training. Today, moonlighting is frowned upon.

Another advantage of a place like Hopkins is exposure to truly varied populations. I could sit down and talk at length with an Arctic explorer, or kibitz with a state or U.S. legislator. People living in poverty, including those who were homeless, had extraordinary stories to tell. Dealing with gypsy clans or Mafia members could be trying. Holding hands across cultures through innumerable fears and getting thankfulness in return was intensely rewarding. It also educated me for the future.

Leaving Hopkins after five years, toward the end of the Vietnam War, I was inducted into the U.S. Army as a major, spending two years on active duty. I did research at Edgewood Arsenal in Maryland, working mostly on antidotes to nerve agents and providing education to other government services. I ran the Toxic Emergency Services, created a cancer screening program for the base, and self-taught myself microsurgery, transplanting mice kidneys under a microscope. This was at the dawn of microsurgery.

The best decision of my life was to live in Annapolis. I got an instructor's appointment at Johns Hopkins while doing private practice in Annapolis and Glen Burnie nearby. It was also a sailing mecca. The two area hospitals were culturally very different and provided a broad spectrum of challenges, diverse types of diseases, and wide ranges of patient personality types and education levels. My Hopkins training allowed me to establish my cancer surgery and my new microscopic surgery, doing firsts in several types of cases.

Over the course of forty-five years, I have taken care of thousands of patients and done thousands of surgeries, small and large. I have undertaken all the types of urologic cancer, referring some of the more difficult ones to Johns Hopkins. Intermingled with these were the basic cases, the nerve and brain urology problems, children's birth defects, and others. The variety is bewildering, and no case is exactly the same. Coupled with this is the fun of learning new technologies to provide better care. It all comes together when sitting at the bedside of an ICU patient throughout a night of worry, recognizing an acutely deathly problem, and rescuing that patient, or holding the hands of a dying patient or his family.

Medicine is a tricky business. A doctor must know the background of their patients, and perceive their mental conditions, as well as their physical diseases. I missed a pathological, emotional attachment to me once, when I successfully repaired a patient's delicate physical problem. I only found out later that he had been discharged from the army for psych reasons. I discharged him from my practice when his physical problem was repaired. But he perceived that as rejection, which led him to sneak up outside my car and put a bullet through the dense window. Shrapnel bashed the side of my head. I fell over and played dead to escape a follow-up bullet.

Only once did I get sued. The patient had a medical problem that at trial was proven not to be related to me, or to the internist. Preparing for that was one year of emotional hell. Oddly, afterward, the patient wanted to come back under my care.

I also testified as an expert witness in a few malpractice trials. During one in particular, I salvaged the truth by again searching the literature for rare cases, and I found one that perfectly applied. The stories are endless. Unusual anatomy or pathologies require on-the-spot, very difficult resolutions. Newer instruments that fail have to be sent back to companies with ideas for redesign. There are also unexpected times, like the surgeon down the operating corridor calling for sudden urologic help -- a quick step into the unknown in the middle of the night. Or more recently, my daughter caught Covid, and then she went into long Covid. She relied on me for advice and treatment, because no one knew much about the disease, and most were so busy caring for the severely acute or dying. I did my homework like no other. I worried over her as my father had worried over me: might I lose her? But she has survived.

The time, effort, and expense of becoming a physician requires perseverance and strength. After high school, it took eighteen years to become a urologist and two more to satisfy my Army commitment, before actually practicing medicine on my own. Many doctors end up with half-a-million dollars of debt to get there. I was lucky enough not to face that. The days in training are more like 24/7 than the normal eight hours a day, five days a week. There's a lot of sleep deprivation. And you have to make straight A's all the way along. The volume of what must be learned and immediately used is mind-boggling. And it is constantly changing throughout your career, which means you are in for lifelong learning across many fields.

The practice from which I retired in 2015 has seventeen urologists, with all the supporting help and modern facilities. The practice landscape has changed profoundly over time. In the 1970s, I charged reasonable fees, took all comers, and gave about 25 percent of my care as charity. It all balanced out. Hospitals stood alone and charged appropriately. Insurance companies were mostly nonprofit. It all changed once the for-profit motive hit these institutions. Costs became squeezed. Corporatization of hospitals and insurance companies and the government have now taken over the gift of medicine, with enumerable rationalizations, to the detriment of the patient and the doctor. The balance has been lost.

Throughout my life I have truly been blessed. I mentioned my father and his side of the family. My mother was made of all love. Without her, my lucky life would not have happened. She had lost her parents early in life but was fortunate to have supportive step-parents. She earned a graduate degree in the history of art in New York and Europe in the 1930s, spoke several languages, and met my father in Vienna. She had grown up skiing and sailing in Seattle. Moving to my father's home in Memphis and Mississippi, she suffered the shocks of Southern cultural changes gracefully. She gave us total support and direction throughout her children's lives.

The greatest downer in my life was my divorce from my first wife. I met her in Sweden, and she patiently endured part of my medical school, internship, and residency, and my "marriage" to my profession. Our personality differences, my continued absences and lack of attention, our lack of funds, and a young child were too much stress on our marriage. I am greatly sorry. Fortunately, now the culture around the medical profession that created so much pressure on us all seems to be improving.

The other important grace in my life was having found my second wife, Brenda, and creating the family we have. I met her several years after starting my practice in Annapolis on an adjacent tennis court. From there we connected on dancing, music, sailing, cooking, and skiing, and I admired her astute intellectual capacity. She was doing educational research for the American Federation of Teachers and had already had a presidential appointment to the Sallie Mae Board. She was personally hosted for lunch by President Carter and Rosalyn Carter at the White House. She gave all this up to raise a family. She took on the job of helping my elder son from my prior marriage grow up, especially with some learning disabilities. She did an incredible job raising all three children. One went to

Chapman University and to Navy Seal school. Two finished at Princeton, with many honors.

The downside is that I didn't share as much time as I should have due to my professional obligations, a loss both to her and to me, especially in those early years of our children's development. But later, we traveled the world together, often with the children, skiing, bareboating and diving in the Caribbean, exploring ancient ruins, visiting museums and art galleries, camping, riding river rapids, horseback riding at a dude ranch, shooting sporting clays, playing tennis, racing sailboats, water skiing, fishing, and being with friends. I learned to make more time for that after I finally reached that stage in my life where I had some control. I now have five grandchildren and family life is fun. Although, recently I have been sequestered at home with immune weakness, avoiding Covid, in spite of my being vaccinated.

Just recently, the fourth recurrence of my tumor has forced me into the last attempted fight with this protagonist. National Institutes of Health does remarkable research on diseases, new approaches, and treatments. I was accepted into a Phase II trial for immunotherapy. It allows a release of my own immune system to freely attack the tumor, and it has worked for several other cancers so far. However, in the process, autoimmune antibodies are released that can attack many of my own organs, which it did in me. Some weeks into treatment I suddenly developed a rapid heartbeat of 230 sustained beats per minute. My ER doctor was a heavenly vision, to say the least. I whispered to her, let me go if that's what happens, as I would rather go this way than through the cancer. But I am still here, so far.

I am making sure I have all the loose ends of my departure all tidied up. I am slowly making the rounds saying goodbye in an indirect way -- letting people know the value of their friendship to me. I guess to some extent I am setting an example for those around me to celebrate me and not mourn or suffer through my departure. I still live each day to its fullest, very happy to still be here, and not dwelling on the end. When all this is done, and with good faith, I think there is no real fear. I was lucky to be here and it was a good life, I have shared my love. Here too, the ability to say goodbye as a whole, normal-appearing person to my children and friends is very important. The problem, of course, lies in the nature of a terminal disease. Medical palliation has been a boon, but it doesn't suffice in many cases. It makes complete ethical sense to provide medicinal termination when those scenarios are expected. It confers dignity and a comforting way to say goodbye. I believe it is the individual's right to make this decision, and it is a travesty many religions and governments can't see this. This is not suicide or rebuking the sanctity of life.

This afternoon after a sudden dark squall, the sky turned pure blue. The sun was a crisp golden, slanting through the new spring leaves with the raindrops still on them, sparkling like diamonds. The returning birds were singing away. Rising up on my crutches, my mind went to this amazingly beautiful creation in which God has placed us. From a single source of energy, through the simple forms of molecules, to the infinity of the universe, here I stand in perhaps the middle of this unknowable miracle -- this life.

Jimmy and Brenda Biles, 2013

Jimmy Biles, 2022

Authors' Zoom Call, 2022